CONTENTS

CHAP.		PAGE
I.	THE NEW MACHINE: TAKING OVER, STARTING-UP AND RIDING HINTS	1
II.	THE THEORY OF THE INTERNAL COMBUSTION ENGINE	17
III.	CARBURATION: ROUTINE MAINTENANCE AND TUNING HINTS	27
IV.	LUBRICATION: ROUTINE TASKS AND MAINTENANCE HINTS	34
V.	LIGHTING AND ELECTRICAL FITTINGS	51
VI.	BICYCLE PARTS: ADJUSTMENTS AND DISMANTLING	71
VII.	MECHANICAL ADJUSTMENTS	90
VIII.	OVERHAULING: DISMANTLING AND RE-ASSEMBLY PROCEDURE	102
IX.	1946 AND 1949 TRIUMPH MODELS	121
X.	FAULTS AND THEIR DIAGNOSIS	131
	INDEX	137

FLOYD CLYMER'S MOTORCYCLIST'S LIBRARY

The Book of the
TRIUMPH

A COMPLETE GUIDE FOR OWNERS AND PROSPECTIVE PURCHASERS OF TRIUMPH MOTOR-CYCLES (1935–1949)

BY

E. T. BROWN, F.L.S.

AUTHOR OF
"*The Owner Driver's Handbook*," "*The Complete Motor-Cyclist*,"
"*The Practical Motor-Cyclist*"

REVISED BY

A. C. DAVIES

Press Contributor on Motoring, Tractors, Power-Farming Equipment, etc.

ANNOUNCEMENT

By special arrangement with the original publishers of this book, Sir Isaac Pitman & Son, Ltd., of London, England, we have secured the exclusive publishing rights for this book, as well as all others in THE MOTORCYCLIST'S LIBRARY.

Included in THE MOTORCYCLIST'S LIBRARY are complete instruction manuals covering the care and operation of respective motorcycles and engines; valuable data on speed tuning, and thrilling accounts of motorcycle race events. See listing of available titles elsewhere in this edition.

We consider it a privilege to be able to offer so many fine titles to our customers.

FLOYD CLYMER
Publisher of Books Pertaining to Automobiles and Motorcycles

2125 W. PICO ST.   LOS ANGELES 6, CALIF.

PREFACE

SINCE the last edition of THE BOOK OF THE TRIUMPH was published a short time ago various interesting features have been incorporated in the three Standard models, the 349 c.c. 3T de Luxe, the 498 c.c. Speed Twin, and the 498 c.c. Tiger "100," while the sporting enthusiast has the choice of two new models, the "Trophy" trials machine and the "Grand Prix" racing machine.

Readers will appreciate that much valuable information was gained from experience during the war years, and it is interesting to note that the Triumph Engineering Company was one of the first to be ready for the change-over from wartime to peace-time production. Of the 1949 range it may be safely said that another page of motor-cycling history has been turned, for these models not only embody unique improvements, but have been designed to present a sleekness of appearance which is second to none.

All alterations have been to the advantage of the rider, and it can be confidently stated that there are no machines more reliable, efficient, comfortable, safe, and economical than the 1949 models. The reliability of the Triumph motor-cycle has always been a household word among the host of enthusiastic riders; so it is not surprising that a very large number of earlier models are still giving faithful service.

In this revised edition of THE BOOK OF THE TRIUMPH every endeavour has been made to anticipate the requirements of the reader, and it is hoped that it will enable riders to obtain not only the best results from their machines, but increase their pleasure on the road owing to trouble-free running. Details regarding design, construction, maintenance, and adjustment given in the following pages refer, in the main, to 1935–49 models inclusive, but owners of previous models will find that much of the advice given applies equally to their mounts.

In conclusion, thanks are tendered to the Triumph Engineering Company for their ready help and courtesy in supplying information and photographs, which were of great assistance in bringing this book up to date.

A. C. D.

INTRODUCTION

Welcome to the world of digital publishing ~ the book you now hold in your hand, while unchanged from the original edition, was printed using the latest state of the art digital technology. The advent of print-on-demand has forever changed the publishing process, never has information been so accessible and it is our hope that this book serves your informational needs for years to come. If this is your first exposure to digital publishing, we hope that you are pleased with the results. Many more titles of interest to the classic automobile and motorcycle enthusiast, collector and restorer are available via our website at www.VelocePress.com. We hope that you find this title as interesting as we do.

NOTE FROM THE PUBLISHER

The information presented is true and complete to the best of our knowledge. All recommendations are made without any guarantees on the part of the author or the publisher, who also disclaim all liability incurred with the use of this information.

TRADEMARKS

We recognize that some words, model names and designations, for example, mentioned herein are the property of the trademark holder. We use them for identification purposes only. This is not an official publication.

INFORMATION ON THE USE OF THIS PUBLICATION

This manual is an invaluable resource for those interested in performing their own maintenance. However, in today's information age we are constantly subject to changes in common practice, new technology, availability of improved materials and increased awareness of chemical toxicity. As such, it is advised that the user consult with an experienced professional prior to undertaking any procedure described herein. While every care has been taken to ensure correctness of information, it is obviously not possible to guarantee complete freedom from errors or omissions or to accept liability arising from such errors or omissions. Therefore, any individual that uses the information contained within, or elects to perform or participate in do-it-yourself repairs or modifications acknowledges that there is a risk factor involved and that the publisher or its associates cannot be held responsible for personal injury or property damage resulting from the use of the information or the outcome of such procedures.

WARNING!

One final word of advice, this publication is intended to be used as a reference guide, and when in doubt the reader should consult with a qualified technician.

CHAPTER I

THE NEW MACHINE: TAKING OVER, STARTING-UP AND RIDING HINTS

THERE are three reasons why the inexperienced motor-cyclist should become fully conversant with the theory and practice of controlling his first machine, whether it be a second-hand pre-war model or a new Triumph model, before attempting to ride it in public. These are: the safety of other road users, the machine and his own safety. Carelessness is the principal cause of road accidents, for it is true that the casual becomes the casualty; lack of road-craft, and an exact knowledge regarding the manipulation of the controls, is also a common cause of accidents in which a motor-cyclist is involved. A motor-cycle is a powerful machine, capable of high speeds; the responsibility of the rider is a heavy one. The new-comer to the sport of motor-cycling is advised to read the whole of this chapter, paying particular attention to the details concerning his own model, before going for the first ride.

Taking over the Machine. The following points should be noted when taking over the machine—

1. See there is a full supply of oil in the various units.

(*a*) There is oil in circuit when the machine is dispatched, but the reservoir is empty. This should be charged to the correct level. The level is 2 in. short of the lip of the filler, in the case of tanks: on the 6/1 model $\frac{1}{2}$ in. lower than the " Full " mark on the dip-stick, the filling point being just below the saddle on the off-side. The small pressure tank close to the gear-box of the 6/1 model should be inspected to see that it contains a full charge of oil, as this is not drained before dispatch, excepting in the case of export. This is purely a precautionary measure.

(*b*) Check the gear oil; the lubricant should be up to the level plug and not the filler plug. This is also a precaution, as full charges are inserted at the factory.

(*c*) See that the lubricant is at a level just showing in the threads of the level plug in the case of models having primary drive oil bath cases.

2. See that the riding position makes for comfort and safety; handlebar and controls, saddle, footrests, and brake pedal all allow for widely variable adjustments.

Handlebars. These are clamped to the forks and their position is adjustable after slackening the clamping bolts. The position of the controls can be easily adjusted, if desired.

Saddle. The height is adjustable by altering position of the anchorage bolts at the base of the coil springs.

Footrests. Variable by slackening tie bolt nuts and engaging the spigot giving desired location. This applies to the 1935–6 models. On 1937–9 Triumphs the footrests are also readily adjustable after loosening the locking nuts. That on the near-side is attached to the oil-bath chain case by means of a peg which engages holes in the case and enables a number of different positions to be obtained. The off-side footrest is fitted to a tapered distance piece and is adjustable for *any* position.

Brake Pedal. The "off" position is determined by the stop screw on the rod arm. After adjusting the stop it is, of course, necessary to adjust the rear brake by means of the hand adjuster.

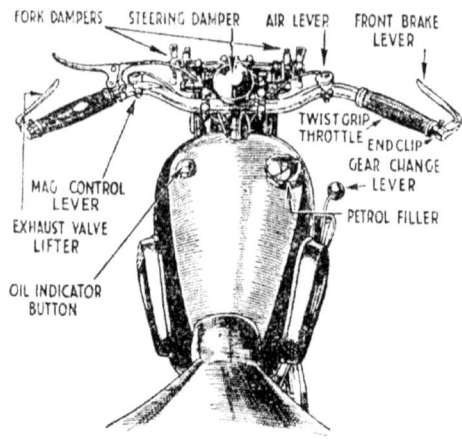

FIG. 1. 1935–6 CONTROLS (SEE FIG. 2)

1946 Models. *Handlebars.* To raise or lower the position of the grips, slacken the four clamping screws securing the caps to the head lug, and rotate handlebar tube as required.

Saddle. Slack off the saddle bolt lock nuts, and adjust the height of the rear of the saddle as required.

Footrests. Tap off the footrests after removing the footrest nuts; the right one is fitted to a taper, and the left one's pegs can be moved round in a series of holes. Tighten up the nuts securely after replacing the footrests in the desired position.

Brake Pedal. The height should be adjusted by means of the stop screw and lock nut in the rear of the brake pedal spindle; adjust the rear brake (see Chapter VI) if necessary.

3. Become familiar with all the controls, their position and operation.

The lay-out of the controls on the 1935–6 models is shown in Fig. 1. On these models the oil pressure is denoted by an indicator button mounted on the petrol tank.

THE NEW MACHINE

The lay-out of the controls on the 1937-9 models is shown in Fig. 2. It will be noted that the ammeter, oil pressure gauge, panel light switch and lighting switch are mounted on the tank panel. As automatic voltage control is provided, there are only three switch positions, namely, "Off," lamps off and dynamo not charging; "L," pilot bulb on, other lamps off, dynamo giving maximum output; and "H," head lamp (main bulb), tail lamp

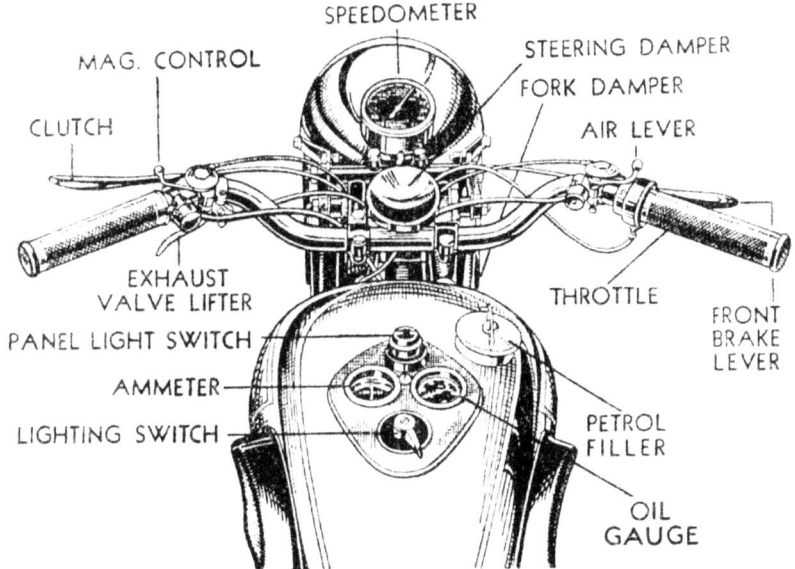

FIG. 2. LAY-OUT OF 1937–9 CONTROLS

On all 1937–9 models the ammeter, oil gauge, and lighting switch are mounted on the tank panel. On some 1935–6 models also an instrument panel is fitted, but this does not include an oil pressure gauge

and sidecar lamp, when fitted, on, and dynamo giving maximum output. The brake pedal is on the left-hand side.

The lay-out of the controls on the 1946 models is shown in Fig. 4. The following details should be noted—

Air Control. This is not fitted on the handlebar as in earlier models; a spring loaded plunger is fitted on the top of the carburettor mixing chamber, for use in very cold weather. To close the control, depress the plunger and turn in a clockwise direction to lock; as soon as the engine warms up, the plunger should be released by turning it anti-clockwise (see Fig. 3).

Cut-out Button. There is a press button located on the left part of the handlebar; this stops the engine by earthing the magneto.

Speedometer. The drive is fitted to the rear wheel, so this must be removed when carrying out bearing adjustments.

Instrument Panel. There are three switch positions, namely, "Off," all lights off; "L," tail and parking lights on; and "H," tail and head lamps on. The charging rate of the dynamo is indicated by the ammeter when the engine is running; the discharge, when the engine is stopped and the lights are on. The rate of charge is not controlled by the switch; this is

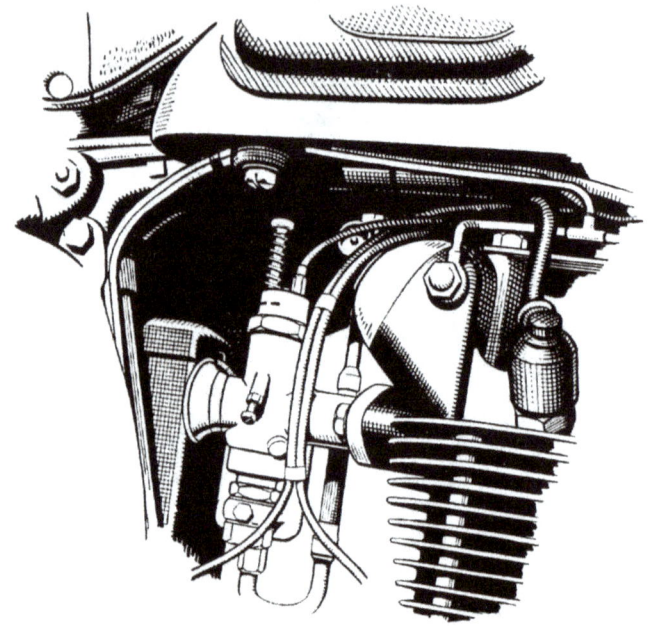

FIG. 3. AIR PLUNGER CONTROL IN OPEN POSITION

governed automatically. Oil pressure to the crankshaft is indicated by the oil pressure gauge.

Controls. The petrol tap is under the rear end of the tank. There are two sources of fuel supply; the main supply is tapped by pulling out the plunger with the circular end. When this supply is exhausted, the hexagonal-ended plunger is pulled out to tap the reserve supply; this is sufficient for about 15 miles running. It is important to note that the main plunger must remain in the "on" position when the reserve plunger is pulled out; otherwise the petrol will not flow from the auxiliary tank. The kick-starter is placed behind the right footrest; the brake pedal in front of the left footrest; the gear change foot lever in front of the right footrest.

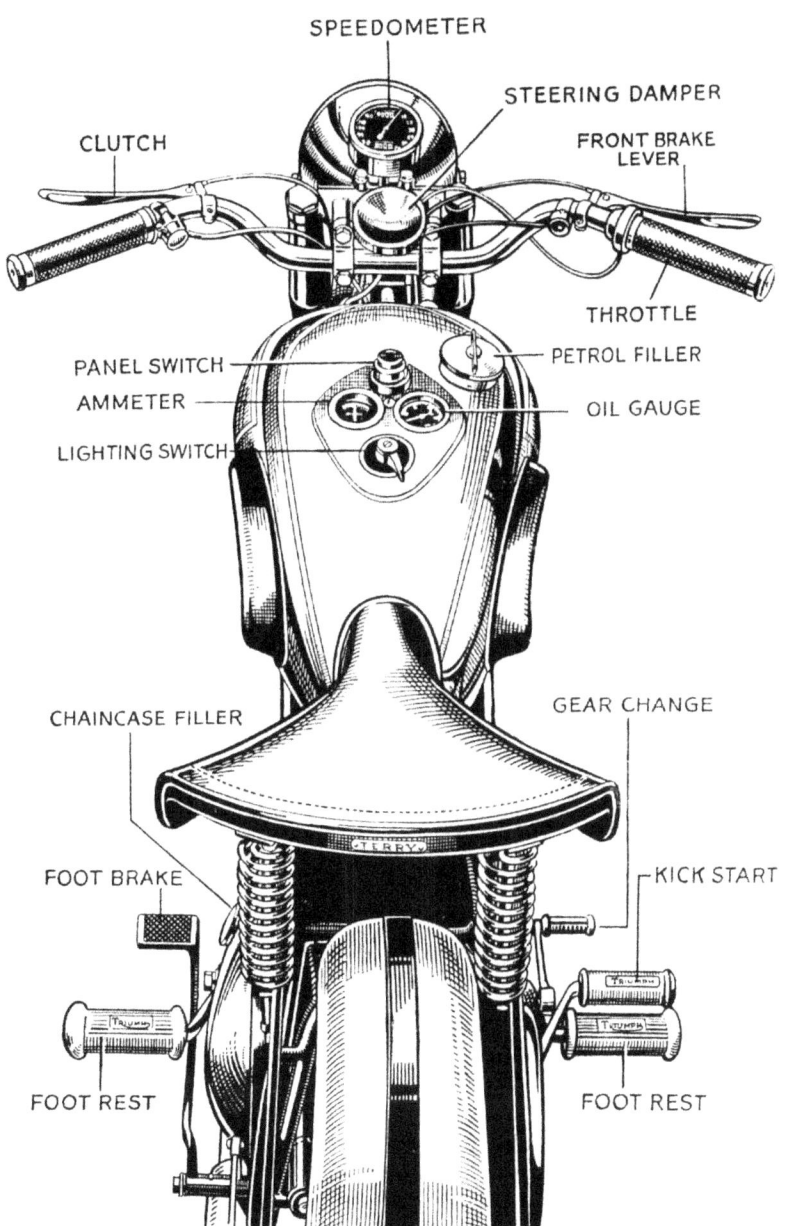

Fig. 4. 1946 Controls

4. See that the battery liquid—the electrolyte—immerses the plates. Important—If the battery is not prepared for charging or is disconnected, keep the switch in the " off " position.

5. It is advisable to slacken off the steering and fork dampers; these are unnecessary at low speeds, while the adjustment of the fork dampers to suit the weight of the rider can easily be carried out later on the road.

6. Check tyre pressures in accordance with data given in Chapter VI.

7. Fill up with petrol; see that the air vent in the filler cap is clear.

1947-8 and 1949 Models. The three standard models, the 349 c.c. 3T de Luxe, the 498 c.c. Speed Twin and the 498 c.c. Tiger "100," for the current season have been improved and brought up to date in various directions, and the two new 1949 Models, the 498 c.c. "Trophy" Trials machine and the "Grand Prix" Racing machine, incorporate the same advancements.

Of outstanding interest is the introduction of the Triumph instrument "Nacelle," an illustration of which is shown in Fig. 5.

This unique panel groups all the instruments and switchgear in an ideal position where they can be most easily seen and used. Built integral with the top of the telescopic forks and, therefore, fully sprung, the nacelle incorporates the headlamp (with adjustable rim), speedometer, ammeter, lighting switch, cut-out button and horn. All instruments are rubber mounted, internally illuminated and readily accessible. This new feature not only improves the appearance of the machine as a whole, but offers many important advantages readily apparent to the hard-riding motor-cyclist.

Starting-up. For 1935-9 models proceed as follows: Place the gear lever in neutral (indicator, foot change); turn on the fuel and depress the tickler until fuel just shows at the base of the mixing chamber, but do not flood the carburettor; place the ignition lever to three-quarters advance—the advance position is towards the rider. Close the air lever and, with a slight throttle opening and with the exhaust lifter lever raised, operate the kick starter. Do this twice, and at the third time release the exhaust lever as the crank reaches the end of its movement. The engine should fire. Allow the kick-starter crank to return immediately to the free position, fully advance the ignition and open the air control wide on single-cylinder models. On twin-cylinder engines it is usually necessary to warm the engine up a little before giving full air, but this should be done as soon as possible. An over-rich mixture is indicated by black smoke issuing from the exhaust.

THE NEW MACHINE

No exhaust valve lifter is provided on the vertical twin, and to facilitate starting the kick-starter crank should be moved to a horizontal position with the aid of the clutch before kicking the engine over. On the 1938-9 coil ignition models, do not forget that the engine cannot start until the ignition is switched on with the ignition key situated in the centre of the lighting switch. A red warning lamp on the instrument panel lights up when the

Fig. 5. Triumph Instrument "Nacelle"

ignition is on and goes out when the engine is speeded up. On no account leave the ignition on with the engine stationary, otherwise a "flat" battery is likely to result.

Allow the engine to tick over for a few seconds in order to verify the oil distribution. This can be done by removing the tank filler cap and noting the delivery of the lubricant from the return pipe immediately inside. Also observe that the oil pressure button, mounted on the tank, is protruding. In the case of 6/1 model, the former evidence is not available, proper circulation being shown by the button movement. On the L2/1 model, the order is reversed, and as no pressure button is used, tank return is conclusive evidence.

An oil pressure gauge instead of an indicator button is provided on the instrument panels of 1937–9 models and a watchful eye must be kept on the gauge to ensure that the lubrication system is functioning correctly. The mere fact that oil is observed being returned to the tank is not proof, on the twin-cylinder models, that the big-ends are receiving adequate lubrication. With regard to the oil pressure, the exact reading varies somewhat and the essential condition is that it should be *steady* and not fluctuate. If the pressure fluctuates or no gauge reading is shown, stop the engine *at once* and investigate. High readings are normal with a cold engine, but they should decrease as the engine warms up. Minimum safe readings for the singles and "Speed Twins" are 5 lb. and 35 lb. per sq. in. respectively. These pressures should be registered with the engine hot and ticking-over.

A rather different procedure is advisable when starting-up a 1946 Triumph. The engine is easy to start, but if the controls are not properly set, a little trouble may be experienced. The following settings are suggested—

See that the gear is located in the neutral position (note indicator on gear-box). Lift the clutch and depress the kick-starter to separate the plates. Close the air control on the top of the carburettor; it is only necessary to use the air control plunger in very cold weather. Turn on the petrol and flood the carburettor by depressing the tickler; experience tells the degree of flooding necessary, but on no account should the tickler be depressed until the fuel flows in a constant stream from the air holes in the top of the float chamber. Open the throttle about four "clicks" on the twist-grip (this opens inwards). Then turn the engine over by means of the kick-starter until compression is felt; it is best to move the kick-starter crank down to a horizontal position by freeing the clutch. Finally, give the kick-starter a long swinging kick, when the engine should start immediately. A second or third attempt may be necessary if the controls are not set in the right position.

Allow the engine to warm up before releasing the air control, but it is highly important to open the air control as soon as possible. Watch the oil pressure gauge when starting up; a pressure of 35 lb. per square inch should register with the oil hot and the machine running at 35 m.p.h. If no pressure is registered the engine must be stopped at once and the cause ascertained and remedied. (See Chapter IV.)

THE NEW MACHINE

Lubrication of the three standard models and the two new 1949 models is somewhat different from that of the 1946 and earlier machines.

The lubrication system employed on the Twin machines is extremely reliable, and it has been possible to dispense with the oil gauge and substitute an oil indicator on the oil pressure release valve.

When the engine is started up it will be seen that the indicator plunger moves out. The rider should see that the indicator is projecting before riding away. It is not necessary continually to check up on the indicator. If the indicator does not project when the engine is started it should be stopped immediately and the trouble investigated.

Some riders who have owned machines fitted with oil gauges for many years may feel that there is "something missing" without this instrument. These riders are reminded that during the war more than 400,000 motor-cycles were manufactured for the armed forces, and none of these was fitted with oil gauges or indicators. Many cars, some selling at high prices, have no indicator to show that the lubricant is circulating. The fact is that the reliability of modern engineering methods has made this fitment obsolete.

Running-in. The life of the motor cycle is reduced considerably if it is handled carelessly during the initial stages of running; hence some space is devoted to a discussion of the subject. To allow the bearing surfaces to harden and bed down, running-in should be carried out progressively. When intelligently and carefully handled, a machine will be faster, mechanically quieter, and will wear longer than the mount of a rider who pays no attention to the finer points which should be considered in running-in.

The fact of paramount importance is that the engine must never be stressed; the best indication of this is the throttle opening. In other words, the engine must not be allowed to labour in the higher gear ratios; changing down to a lower gear certainly causes the engine to rev faster, but much more easily. For the first 250 miles not more than a quarter throttle opening should be used.

To enable the rider to judge the throttle opening, it is suggested that a little spot of white paint should be put on the twist-grip rubber, and a spot of black paint on the chromium-plated twist-grip body, in such a position that these coincide when the throttle is closed, or the white spot can be located at a quarter throttle opening, and altered later as an increased opening is desirable. When this mileage has been covered, the throttle opening can be increased to one-third, and progressively afterwards until full throttle opening is allowable when about 1200 miles are registered on the speedometer.

It is suggested that the rider of a new Triumph should amble along at a comparatively slow speed throughout the running-in period. Speed bursts are desirable occasionally. If the machine easily reaches, say, 50 m.p.h. with a certain throttle opening, on the first occasion the engine should be throttled down; after a period of slower running 50 m.p.h. may be reached again and held on to for a little longer. By working up gradually in this way the time will come when the first of a few miles at 50 m.p.h. has been arrived at progressively. The same care should be exercised when higher speeds are attained later on during the running-in period. Work up to maximum speed very carefully and hold it for short, but ever-increasing, periods initially. At really high speeds, it is advantageous to close the throttle momentarily at regular intervals during the running-in period, as this allows an increased amount of oil to pass up the cylinder bore. This precaution is not, of course, necessary when the engine has been thoroughly run-in.

Normal Running. With the engine started, the machine may be put into motion. To engage low gear, depress the clutch lever to its limit, pausing a few seconds to allow the plates to separate. With "wet" clutches operating in an oil bath, a little drag when cold is inevitable, owing to the increased viscosity of the lubricant at lower temperatures, but this can be overcome if the clutch lever is raised and released while respectively accelerating and shutting off engine speed. Then pull the gear lever into low gear position. (See later paragraph if foot control is fitted.) Open the throttle a little and release the pressure on the clutch lever gradually; the engine should take up the drive sweetly and smoothly.

The art of driving can only be learned properly by actual demonstration, but the following suggestions are made—

(a) A good change can only be made when the road wheel speed and engine speed are synchronized. In changing up, this is easy, for steady progress with the clutch withdrawal, throttle closing, and gear lever operation allows the engine to slow down to the required revolutions in accordance with the wheel movement. When changing down, accelerate a little after pressing the clutch lever, going on to gear lever as quickly as possible, with immediate clutch release in both cases.

(b) Always drive on the throttle and never on the clutch or the brakes. Keep the fingers right away from the clutch lever and the foot well away from the brake pedal.

(c) Only use the clutch for starting, stopping, and gear changing.

THE NEW MACHINE

Never slip the clutch on hills in an attempt to relieve the load on the engine. If it is necessary to stand for any appreciable time with the engine running, engage neutral.

(d) It is always better if hills can be taken at speed, but if this is impossible, owing to conditions or surface, change down early while the machine still has a good speed.

(e) Do not operate the exhaust lifter when changing gear. The action of the foot gear control is positive; a full stroke of the lever movement engages next adjacent gear only in whichever direction it is operated. That is, the lever is always moved downwards from rest to limit of travel for lower gear than that engaged, and upwards for higher gear position. Releasing the lever allows automatic reloading for the next operation.

The gear positions are indicated by a pointer on the control lever, registering with marks on the body. The lever is radially adjusted through approximately 18 degrees. Neutral is best engaged by changing right down to low gear, when a slight touch on the lever will readily find the intermediate position, or, locating by hand with the visual aid of the pointer.

With the 1946-9 Triumphs the gear lever should be moved down to change down, and up to change up. To select neutral, withdraw the clutch and move the gear lever three movements down and half a movement up. To engage first gear from neutral, fully withdraw the clutch and press the gear lever down one movement. To change up, close the throttle, fully withdraw the clutch, pause for a moment, then move the lever upwards gently as far as it will go with the toe. To change down, fully withdraw the clutch, and press the lever downwards as far as it will go.

The 1946-9 engines are designed for use with an anti-knock fuel. Pool petrol is being employed until such time as these fuels are available; in order to prevent pinking judicious use of the throttle and gears is essential.

In the case of the improved 3T de Luxe, the Speed Twin, the Tiger "100," and the "Trophy" and "Grand Prix" models, a patented positive stop foot-changer is standard. This is fully enclosed.

Stopping. To come to a standstill close the throttle, disengage the clutch and gently apply the foot brake. The engine need not be stopped for a traffic block, but the throttle should be closed sufficiently to allow the engine to "tick over" quietly. The gear lever should be moved to the low gear position as the machine comes to rest so that low gear is engaged in readiness for moving off from stationary. If the engine is stopped the gear lever should be placed into neutral position.

Steering. Steering a motor-cycle when ridden solo is no more difficult than riding an ordinary bicycle, excepting that one is dealing with a machine that is considerably heavier; hence the need for more care in maintaining absolute control. When riding a combination outfit, however, steering is rendered rather different, in that there is always a drag on the cycle in accordance with the precise alignment of the combination. When taking a left-hand corner the tendency is for the sidecar to leave the road, but this difficulty is overcome by reducing the speed and leaning well over to the near-side.

TRAFFIC REGULATIONS

The general laws in connexion with traffic regulations and other points relative to motor-cycling should be fully grasped at the outset. The following are the most important.

In this country all vehicles must keep to the left or near-side of the road. When overtaking another vehicle this should be left on the rider's near-side; on-coming vehicles are passed on their off-side. The only exception to this is in the case of a led horse, in which case it is allowed to occupy the off-side of the road; hence it must be passed on the near-side when overtaking and the off-side when meeting it. This allows the leader of the horse to have complete control of his charge. In most places tramcars may be passed on either side; in certain localities, however, there are by-laws to the effect that either one side or the other is prohibited.

A copy of the Highway Code has been sent to every house in the country; it should be carefully studied. Failure to observe any provision of the code is not at present a ground for criminal proceedings of any kind. Nevertheless, it may be relied upon as tending to establish or negative liability in connexion with any other proceedings, whether civil or criminal.

Speed Limit. Under Section 1 of the Road Traffic Act, 1934, it is an offence to exceed a speed of 30 miles per hour on—

(a) A road provided with street lamps, or

(b) A road to which the speed limit has been applied by Order. The speed limit sign is shown at No. 1, top, in Fig. 6.

Certain roads, although lighted, have been freed from the speed limit by Order. In such cases No. 2 sign (Fig. 6, top) is fixed to the lamp posts.

The more important of the traffic signs are shown in Figs. 6 and 7; the motor-cyclist should make himself familiar with their significance.

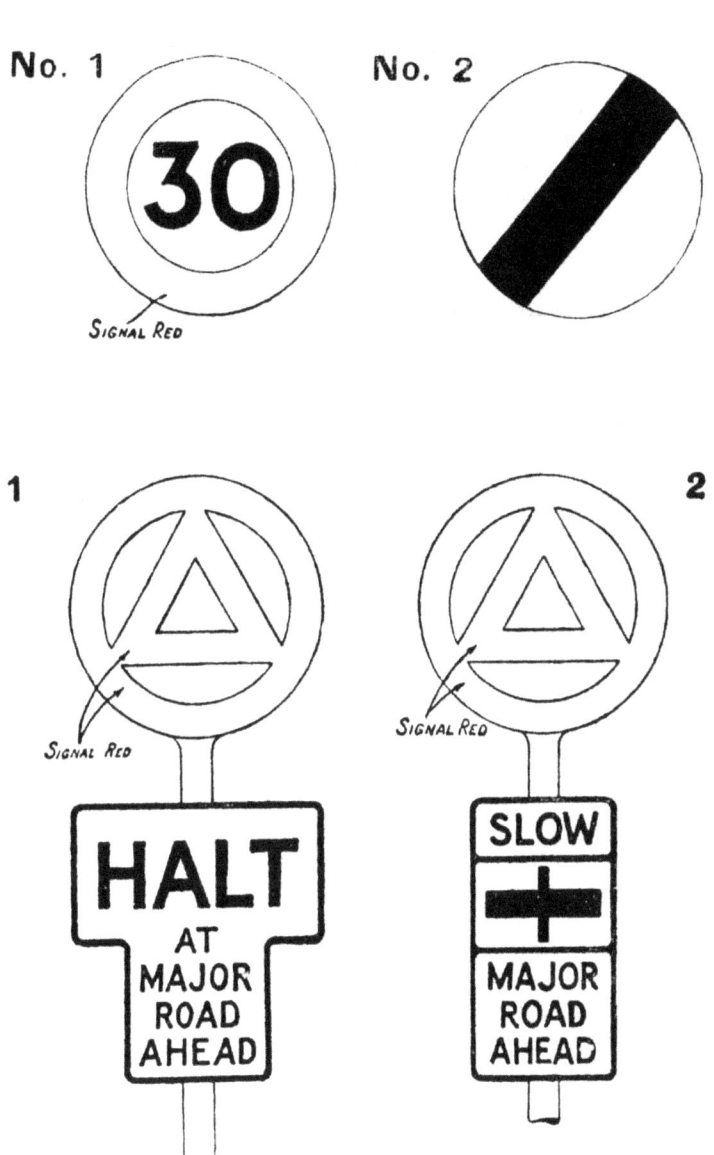

Fig. 6. Important Road Signs
(*By courtesy of H.M. Stationery Office*)

Lights. Between half an hour after sunset and half an hour before sunrise on the public highway a solo motor-cycle must carry one white light in front and a red light at the rear, together with proper illumination of the rear number-plate. Motor-cycles with sidecars attached must carry two white lights in front and a red light showing to the rear, together with proper illumination of the rear number-plate. During summer time the half hour period is extended to one hour.

Silencers. All motor-cycle engines must be reasonably silent. The law is not very explicit in this connexion as regards the amount of noise that may be emitted, but it may be taken that all Triumph models are sufficiently silenced to meet the requirement of the law. No form of cut-out may be used; that is, a device which allows the exhaust gases to pass direct to the air without first going through the silencer.

Brakes. A motor-cycle must be fitted with two independent brakes, but these may be fixed either one to each wheel or both to the rear wheel. Each brake must, however, be sufficiently powerful to pull up the motor-cycle within a short distance.

Audible Warning. Some warning device must be fitted to the motor-cycle so that other road users may be made aware of the approach of a vehicle. A bulb horn is sufficiently powerful for town work, but an electric or hand-operated horn is better for country riding, as it is not always easy to make drivers of commercial vehicles hear an ordinary bulb horn. However, on all 1939-49 models with electric lighting equipment, an electric horn is fitted as standard. It should be particularly noted that it is now illegal to sound the horn (*a*) when the machine is stationary, (*b*) between the "silence" hours of 11.30 p.m. and 7 a.m.

Pedestrian Crossings. Pedestrians using crossings indicated by studs on the road and "Belisha" beacons have *absolute* right of way, though they must not loiter. It is an offence to refuse right of way to a pedestrian or to stop on a crossing.

The Speedometer. Every motor-cycle whose capacity exceeds 100 c.c. must have a speedometer fitted to indicate the correct speed within a 10 per cent margin.

Smooth Tyres. It is illegal to-day to continue to run a machine after the tyre treads have worn smooth. So do not try economizing in this direction, otherwise you will have to economize in other directions!

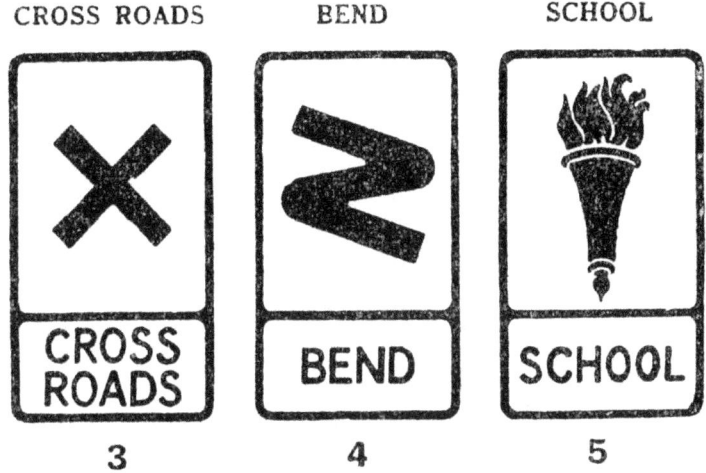

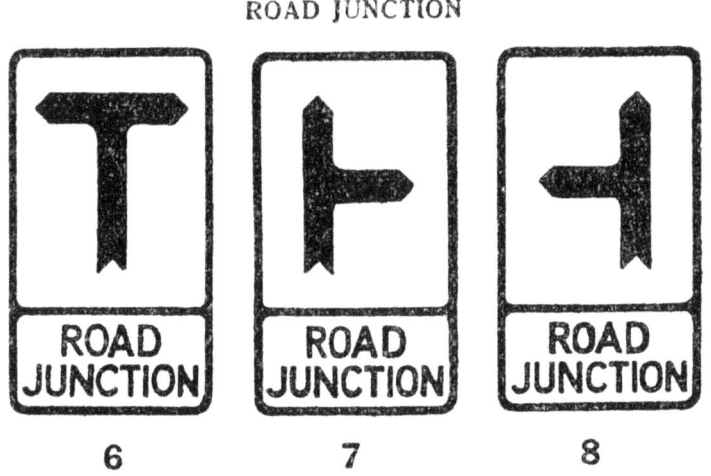

Fig. 7. Important Road Signs
(*By courtesy of H.M. Stationery Office*)

The Pillion Passenger. Where a pillion passenger is carried he (or more probably she) must ride *astride* the machine on a seat *fixed* to the motor-cycle.

Mascots. Mascots of a nature or position such that they are liable to cause injury to a pedestrian in the event of collision are illegal.

Parking Off the Highway. It is no longer permissible to *drive* a motor-cycle off the highway and park it in the middle of a common or other public land. You can, however, park it at a distance not exceeding 15 yards from the highway. The only exception is in the case of an emergency (fire, accident, etc.).

The " Halt " Sign. It is compulsory to obey the sign shown at 1, Fig. 6, bottom. Many motor-cyclists have been fined for its disregard. It is not compulsory, though advisable, to obey the "Slow" sign shown in Fig. 6.

Traffic Lights. Disregard of traffic lights is a serious offence. *Red* means "Stop"; *Green* means "Proceed"; *Amber* means "Prepare to stop or proceed," according to whether it follows the green or red respectively.

Obstructions. No motor-cycle or sidecar outfit may be left in a crowded public street or thoroughfare if likely to cause an obstruction. In the majority of towns recognized parking places are available; one of these should always be used. On no account may the machine be left unattended with the engine running.

Petrol Storage. Not more than 60 gallons of petrol in 2-gallon tins may be stored by a motor-cyclist. The store must not be placed within 20 ft. of any building or stack of inflammable material.

CHAPTER II

THE THEORY OF THE INTERNAL COMBUSTION ENGINE

The Mechanism. The internal combustion engine—the type of engine that is employed in motor-cycles and motor-cars—derives its name from the fact that the heat energy latent in the fuel is released inside the cylinder. In the case of the steam engine the heat is generated apart from the engine and conveyed to the cylinder. The internal combustion engine is, therefore, a small, compact, and absolutely self-contained power unit. The engine may be described in general terms as consisting of a cylinder, inside which works a piston in a similar manner to steam engine practice, and a crankcase, inside which is mounted a crankshaft. The piston is connected by means of a stiff rod, the connecting rod placed at right angles to the crankshaft. In this manner the reciprocating or up-and-down motion of the piston is converted into a rotary motion of the crankshaft.

The Component Parts of the Engine. The cylinder is generally made of cast iron, but in some instances steel or steel liners are employed. In form it is tubular and of uniform diameter, one end being closed and the inner surface as smooth as glass. The piston fits closely into the cylinder and may be composed of cast iron, or aluminium alloy. It is similar in shape to the cylinder, with one end closed. It is imperative that the fit of the piston be such that by its downward movement a partial vacuum is formed in the cylinder head. If a plain piston were employed this would be impossible, as the fit would have to be so tight that movement would be impossible. This difficulty is overcome by means of rings, made of springy iron, inserted into grooves in the piston wall. The rings are broken, the ends either being slotted or cut at an angle of 45 degrees. Their natural expansion ensures a gas-tight fit being secured.

In order that the reciprocating or up-and-down motion of the piston may be changed into a rotary motion at the crankshaft, the connecting rod is hinged at the upper end to the piston and at the lower end to the crankpin. The piston connexion is known as the gudgeon pin or small-end bearing; the crankpin connection as the big-end bearing. The small-end bearing generally consists of a plain circular hole or " bush " in which the gudgeon pin works; the form of the big-end bearing varies according to the construction of the machine. When internal flywheels are fitted a roller or a plain bearing is employed, although in some instances a split bearing, similar to that used in motorcars, is fitted. In this case the circular end of the connecting rod is cut through and the two halves are fitted round the crankpin. The bearings may be either of white metal or phosphor bronze and are also cut in halves in the same way. The whole bearing is kept secure by means of two bolts. Oilways are cut in the bearings so that the contacting surfaces may be properly lubricated.

The crankshaft is mounted on ball or roller bearings. The latter type of bearing is now coming into general use in modern O.H.V. engines. The crankshaft is housed in the crankcase, this case being cut longitudinally so that the bearings may be renewed when necessary. Flywheels are fitted to the crankshafts of all internal combustion engines. The object of the flywheels is to store up the energy delivered by the impulse stroke, so that the piston is enabled to travel through the other strokes of the cycle of operations. The weight of the wheels depends largely upon the type of engine, whether two- or four-stroke, and upon the number of cylinders. The upper portion serves as a mounting for the cylinder. All Triumph engines are of the four-stroke type.

The Explosive Mixture. The explosive mixture, composed of from 1 to 14 to 1 to 17 parts of petrol-vapour and air respectively, is produced in the carburettor. The principle of the carburettor may be seen in Fig. 10, which illustrates very clearly the principal characteristics. The explosive mixture is introduced into the combustion chamber, that is, the section of the cylinder above the piston head, either by means of ports as in the two-stroke engine, or valves as in the four-stroke type, by suction on the downward movement of the gas-tight piston. Similar provision is made for the exit of the inert gases which are the product of combustion after firing. The whole question of the regulation of the inlet of the explosive mixture and the expulsion of the exhaust gases is dealt with fully later in the chapter, where the four-stroke internal combustion engine is described.

The Magneto. At a predetermined moment the explosive mixture is fired by means of an electric spark jumping across the gap between the electrodes of the sparking plug which is fitted in the upper part of the combustion chamber. The electric current is generated in a self-contained machine called the magneto. The magneto consists of a number of horse-shoe magnets, between the poles of which an armature is caused to rotate. The armature is composed of a core of soft iron, round which are a few turns of fairly thick wire. These wires cutting through the field of magnetic force between the poles of the

THE INTERNAL COMBUSTION ENGINE

magnets induce a low tension current to be generated. This winding, known as the primary winding, is connected with the contact breaker mounted on the armature shaft. The points of the contact breaker are separated by means of a cam attached to a ring which revolves with the armature. When the points of the contact breaker are opened the circuit of the primary current is broken. A second winding of very thin wire—the secondary winding—is wound round the outside of the primary winding, one end of this being attached to the slip ring, while the other is earthed. At the moment the current is stopped in the primary winding by the action of the contact breaker, a high tension current is induced in the secondary winding, this being collected by the slip ring and conducted to the sparking plug by the high tension lead or cable.

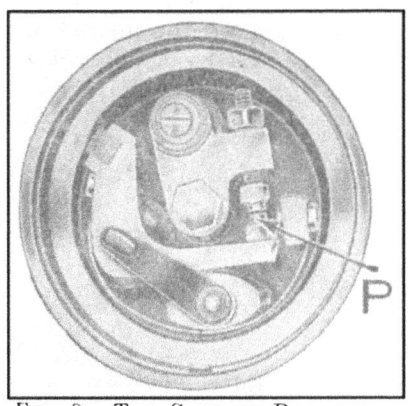

FIG. 8. THE CONTACT BREAKER OF THE MAGNETO

The "break" at P = approx. 1/80 in.

The points of the contact breaker are kept together in the closed position by means of a spring, and are only separated when a spark is due to occur in the combustion chamber. A typical contact breaker is shown in Fig. 8.

As will be understood by reference to page 23, the rotary contact breaker is driven at *half engine speed*. The magneto on all 1935–9 models except those with coil ignition is combined with the dynamo, the complete unit being the Lucas "Magdyno." On 1937 and later "Magdynos" the contact breaker is of different design from that shown in Fig. 8; it is of what is known as the face cam type (see Fig. 9). In this case the whole contact breaker does not rotate. An important component of the magneto (internal) is the condenser whose function is to prevent arcing at the contacts. It does this by preventing a surge of current across them at the moment of the "break."

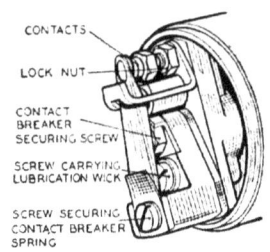

FIG. 9. LUCAS FACE CAM CONTACT BREAKER

On some modern machines such as the 1946–9 Triumphs, the lighting current is generated by a separate dynamo, gear-driven direct from the forward camshaft, and a magneto is employed to supply the spark at the plug points.

Coil Ignition. Coil ignition is provided on the 1938-9 Models 2HC, 3HC. With this system a low-tension current is generated by a dynamo and led to a battery from which current is supplied at an almost constant voltage to the lighting system, and also the coil which like the magneto has a primary and secondary winding. As on the magneto, the current in the primary circuit is interrupted by a contact breaker (attached to the dynamo),

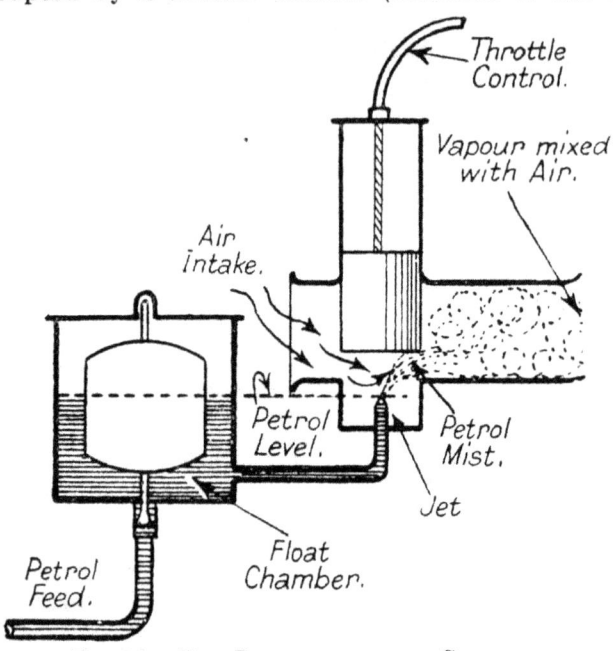

FIG. 10. THE PRINCIPLE OF THE CARBURETTOR

a high-tension current then being induced in the secondary winding and led to the sparking plug. Other features in the system are the ignition switch (which earths the primary circuit), the condenser, and the warning lamp (see page 55).

The Principle of the Carburettor. The function of this very important instrument is to supply the engine at all times with a properly proportioned mixture of air and petrol vapour (in the ratio of 1 to 14 approximately), as previously noted. In Fig. 10 is shown a diagram representing the simplest jet carburation system imaginable. The system is based on the fact that it has been proved that the readiest means of inducing liquid petrol to vaporize rapidly without the application of heat is to split it up into minute particles, or to atomize it, by forcing it through or sucking it through a tube of very fine bore at high speed. This tube is known as the jet, and the level of petrol in the jet is maintained correctly by the action of a sheet copper float in a small fuel reservoir, known as the float chamber, which is fed with fuel from the main tank. When petrol enters the float chamber the level rises by force of gravity until such time as the cone needle valve attached to the float obstructs the further passage of fuel. It does this as soon as the level of petrol corresponds to a level a fraction below the jet orifice. Above the jet are two barrel-shaped chambers communicating with each other, one placed horizontally and one vertically. The horizontal chamber is open to the air at one end, and the other end leads direct into the inlet port of the engine. The open end is known as the air intake. Within, and sliding up and down in the vertical chamber, is a close fitting throttle slide whose up and down movement can be controlled from the handlebars by means of a Bowden cable. When the throttle slide is permitted to descend, the area in which the jet finds itself is greatly restricted and the amount of air that can pass from the air intake across the jet and mix with the atomized petrol vapour is strictly limited for any given instant. The air is drawn in by the violent suction caused when the piston descends in the cylinder and the combustion chamber is in direct communication with the carburettor. Thus it will be seen that as the throttle slide is raised or lowered with the engine in action, so is the volume of explosive mixture supplied to it increased or curtailed thereby. In other words, as we raise or open the throttle so does the power output of the engine increase.

Such, then, is the explanation of the working of a simple carburation system such as that illustrated in Fig. 10. But consider for a moment whether this system which appears sound will work in practice. Actually it will not, for petrol vapour and air are dissimilar vapours and do not respond evenly to varying suctions, and varying suctions there must inevitably be, save in the case of stationary engines provided with governors. In the case of a motor-cycle, the rider is continually altering the strength of the explosive mixture in order to increase or decrease his speed or to combat ever-changing road and weather conditions. Obviously there must be separate control of the air and petrol vapour by the use of two independent slides, one for throttling the air intake and one for throttling the entry to the induction pipe. The various refinements and complications found in all modern carburettors, have, as their purpose—
 1. Simplification of control.
 2. Homogeneous mixing of the air and petrol vapour.
 3. Easy starting.
 4. Flexibility.

22 THE BOOK OF THE TRIUMPH

5. Ability to run at low speed uniformly.
6. Means for enabling special settings to be obtained.
7. Economy.

The Four-stroke Engine. The four-stroke engine is rather more complicated than the two-stroke, in the sense that there

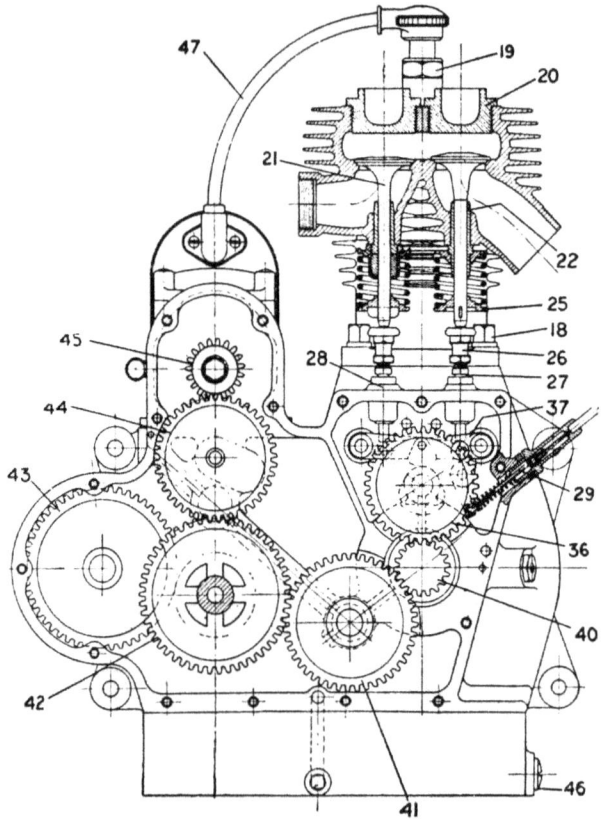

FIG. 11. SECTIONAL VIEW OF 1925 TRIUMPH ENGINE ILLUSTRATING THE FOUR-STROKE PRINCIPLE

are more constituent parts, but this does not mean that it is difficult to maintain this type in efficient working condition. The inlet of the explosive mixture and the expulsion of the exhaust gases are regulated by valves, the poppet valve being the form in general use. The valves and their necessary timing gear consist of a number of different parts, but with occasional attention they may be relied upon to work efficiently for long periods.

THE INTERNAL COMBUSTION ENGINE 23

The working of the poppet valve can best be described with the aid of Fig. 11, which shows a view of the offside of the engine fitted to an old Triumph model with the timing cover removed. The valve, 21, is made with an almost flat head mounted on a long stem. The edge of the head is bevelled, generally at an angle of 45 degrees. The valve head fits into a hole cut in the cylinder casting, the edge of this hole also being

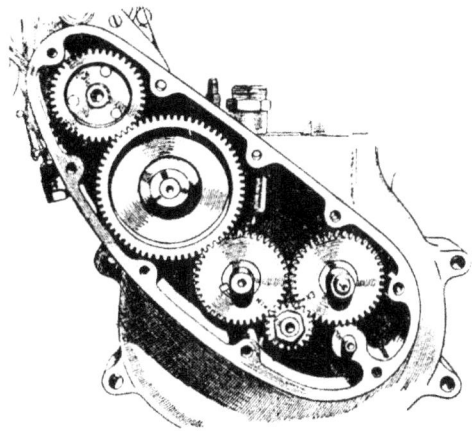

FIG. 12. TIMING GEAR (SINGLE-CYLINDER TRIUMPH)

bevelled to correspond with the valve head. The valve stem passes through the valve guide, 22, in the cylinder casting to the tappet head, 26. The section of the valve stem which is outside the cylinder casting is surrounded by a spring, the function of which is to close the valve. The spring is attached to a cap, which in turn is fixed to the valve by means of a cotter pin, passing through the valve stem, 25. The spring is in a state of compression and pulls the valve down on to its bevelled seating. The valves are opened by means of tappets, 27, which are fitted with adjustable heads, 26, and pass into the crankcase through tappet guides, 28. The tappets are in turn actuated by the cams worked in conjunction with the timing gear (Fig. 12). The cam gear is shown at 36, while the cam rocker lever, the part which actually works the tappets, is shown at 37. As will be seen the cam gear is worked off a pinion attached to the crankshaft, 40, and the cam gear wheel is double the size of the crankshaft pinion, so that each tappet is only actuated once for every second revolution of the crankshaft. The action of the exhaust valve lifter, a device to facilitate starting, can be seen at 29. By means of this valve lifter the exhaust valve may be raised and left slightly open while the kick-starter is being operated; by this means the compression is reduced and the engine is easier to rotate.

The old practice when the poppet valve was employed was to arrange the two valves for each cylinder " side-by-side " or at the side of the cylinder. For many reasons, however, it is now usual

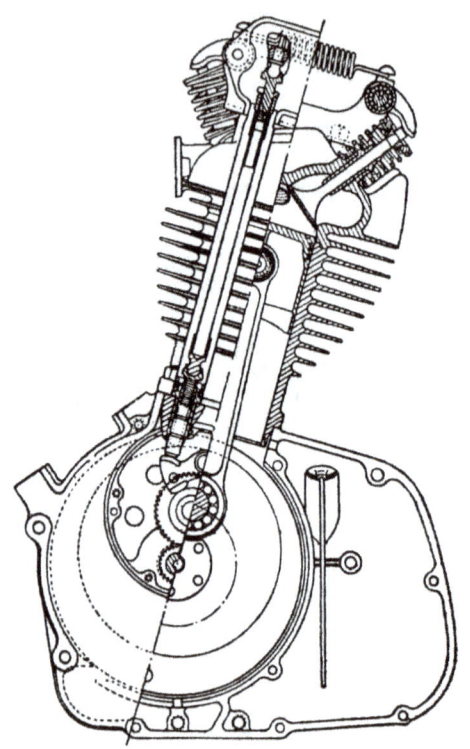

FIG. 13. O.H.V. ENGINE SECTION (EARLY TYPE)

to place the valves in the top of the cylinder head, that is, in the overhead position. There is no doubt that the highest degree of efficiency can be attained in this way. No part of the valve is masked (Fig. 13), while turbulence is not interfered with in any way. In the earlier models of the overhead-valve type, the noise caused by the exposed mechanism was considerable and the wear on the working parts was excessive. These difficulties have, however, been overcome.

The Cycle of Operations. The four-stroke engine, as its name implies, only delivers power with one stroke out of every four.

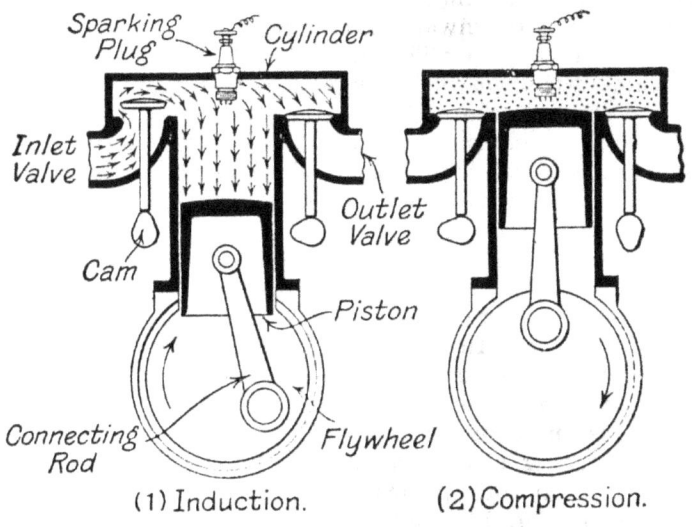
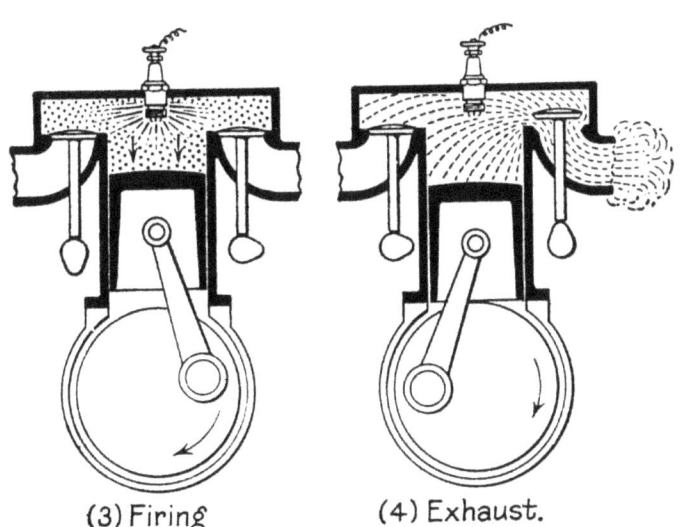

Fig. 14. THE FOUR-STROKE CYCLE

Note the positions of the piston and valves during each of the four strokes.

The four strokes of the cycle of operations are induction, compression, firing, and exhaust. The piston during the induction stroke moves in a downward direction with the inlet valve open, as shown at 1 in Fig. 14. The suction caused by the movement of the gas-tight fitting piston draws the explosive mixture into the combustion chamber through the induction or inlet pipe. So that the explosion may be as forceful as possible, the explosive mixture must be compressed. This is carried out during the next upward movement of the piston, as shown at 2, Fig. 14, both valves being closed meanwhile.

The explosion of the mixture is not instantaneous ; hence the spark is timed to occur, when the engine is " revving " quickly, a fraction of a second before the piston reaches the top of this compression stroke. In this way the full force of the explosion is delivered to the piston head when it is at dead centre ; that is, at the extreme top of its stroke. The result of the explosion causes the piston to move in a downward direction, thus giving the third or firing stroke, as depicted at 3, Fig. 14. On its return journey on the upward stroke the piston drives out the burnt gases, 4, Fig. 14, through the exhaust valve which has been opened for that purpose. When the piston is at the top of the exhaust stroke the exhaust valve closes and the inlet valve opens, when another charge of the explosive mixture is drawn into the combustion chamber. The function of the flywheel is seen here, since were it not for the energy stored up by this wheel the piston would be unable to travel through the exhaust, induction (or inlet), and compression strokes.

CHAPTER III

CARBURATION: ROUTINE MAINTENANCE AND TUNING HINTS

The Triumph Carburettor. The Triumph carburettor is a streamlined, highly efficient instrument. The petrol is first formed into an emulsion of air and petrol before passing into the main choke. The amount of air passing through the primary choke controls the main jet depression and, consequently, the mixture strength. This regulation is obtained by means of a small piston sleeve which, when set for given atmospheric conditions, makes the carburettor fully automatic. An adjustable pilot jet is incorporated to give slow running and easy starting. The fuel supply is regulated by a taper needle which should be adjusted to approximately three-quarters of one complete turn in an anti-clockwise direction from the closed position. The Triumph carburettor fitted to a number of earlier models is extremely reliable and is not likely to give rise to trouble; should anything of the nature develop it is advisable to consult the makers.

The Amal Carburettor. All 1935-9 Triumph models are fitted with an Amal carburettor. Its working is described in detail. When the petrol tap is turned on, the fuel flows past the needle valve U, Fig. 15, until sufficient has entered the chamber R to raise the float T, at which stage the needle valve prevents a further supply entering the float chamber. The action of the float is as follows: As the quantity of fuel in the float chamber is consumed, the float T drops, carrying with it the needle U, and a further supply is admitted. In this way the petrol level is kept constant automatically. Readers are warned that no alteration should be made to the standard setting.

When the float chamber is filled to the correct level, the fuel passes along the passages, through the diagonal holes in the jet plug Q, and is then in communication with the main jet P and the pilot feed hole K. The level in these jets is the same as that maintained in the float chamber.

When the throttle valve B is opened very slightly, and the piston is descending, a partial vacuum is created in the carburettor. This causes a rush of air through the pilot air-hole L and draws fuel from the pilot jet J. The mixture of air and fuel is admitted to the engine through the pilot outlet M. The quantity of mixture which can be passed by the pilot outlet M is insufficient to run the engine, while this mixture also carries an excess of fuel. Before a

28 THE BOOK OF THE TRIUMPH

combustible mixture is admitted, throttle valve *B* must be slightly raised, so that a further supply of air is admitted from the main air intake.

The further the throttle is opened, the less is the depression on

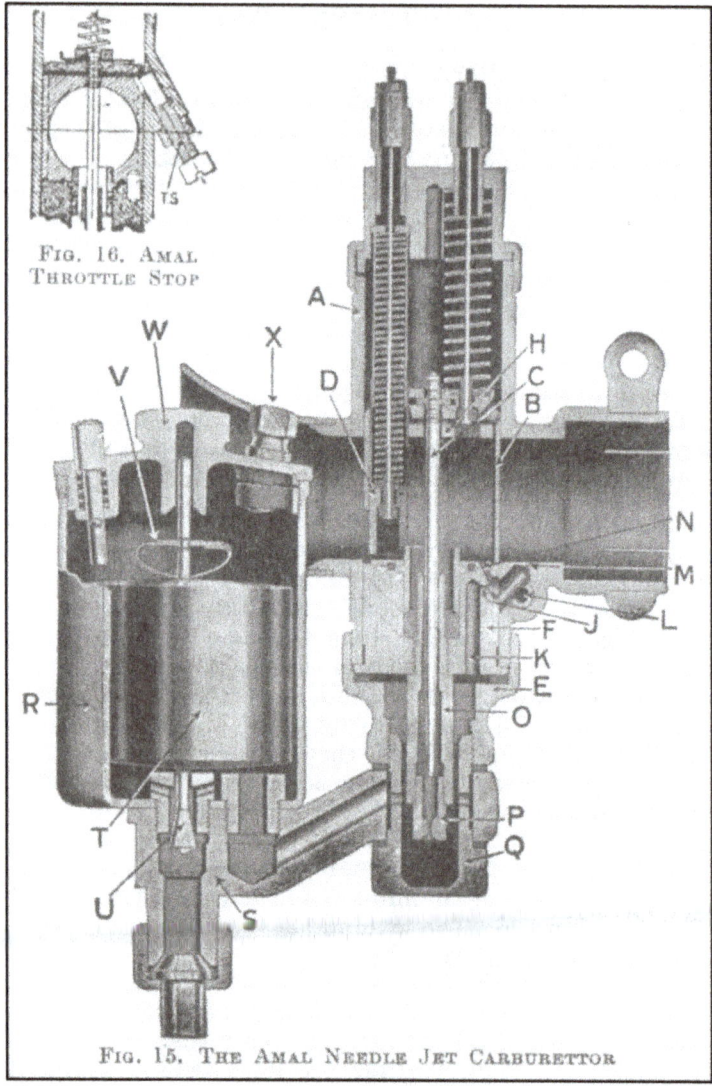

Fig. 16. Amal Throttle Stop

Fig. 15. The Amal Needle Jet Carburettor

the outlet *M* but, in turn, a higher depression is created on the by-pass *N*, so the pilot mixture flows from this passage as well as from the outlet *M*. The mixture provided by the pilot and by pass system is supplemented at approximately one-eighth throttle by fuel from the main jet system, the throttle cut-away governing the mixture strength from this point to one-quarter throttle. Proceeding up the throttle range, mixture control by the position of the needle takes place from one-quarter to three-quarter throttle, and thereafter the main jet is the only regulation. The air valve D, which is cable-operated on the two-lever carburettor, has the effect of obstructing the main throughway and, in consequence, the depression on the main jet is increased, thus enriching the mixture.

Maintenance of the Amal Carburettor. The carburettor should be cleaned occasionally if it is to maintain its efficiency. It should be entirely dismantled and each part washed in clean petrol. In carrying out this operation the following points should be remembered: If the jet block is tight, it may be tapped out by means of a wooden stump in the mixing chamber. All worn parts should be renewed, such as the needle valve, if the head has a distinct ridge at the point of seating; the throttle valve, if there is excessive side play; the mixing chamber union nut washer, if this is worn or damaged; and the taper needle and clip, if the needle can be rotated freely in the clip. To clear the passages a fine bristle should be inserted.

Brute force should never be used when assembling the carburettor. Make certain that the taper needle is refitted in the correct groove and securely locked by the clip; see that it enters the central hole in the top of the jet block; note that the needle valve enters the top of the float chamber cover easily; make sure that the mixing chamber is fitted vertical and pushed right home on the engine stub; see that the washer is in good condition, if flange fitting to the cylinder; that the needle valve clip V registers correctly in the groove; and re-set the pilot adjusting screw.

Stretch in the Bowden wire can be taken up by means of the screwed abutments at the top of the body of the carburettor. Idle movement of both air and throttle controls should be eliminated as far as possible, but it is a simple matter to arrange for the movement of the slide to be coincident with the turning of the lever or the grip, as the case may be.

Tuning the Amal Carburettor. The quality of the mixture supplied can be varied in four ways: (1) main jet (three-quarters to full throttle); (2) pilot air adjustment (closed to one-eighth throttle); (3) throttle valve cut-away on the air intake side (one-eighth to one-quarter throttle); and (4) needle position (one-quarter to three-quarters throttle).

When the carburettor has been carefully assembled and fitted, its general tuning can be carried out.

1. *Obtain the Main Jet Size.* This is done by selecting the

smallest size jet which will give maximum speed, the air lever being three-quarters open.

2. *Pilot Air Adjustment.* To weaken the slow-running mixture, screw the pilot air adjuster outwards. To enrich the slow-running mixture, screw the pilot air adjuster inwards. Screw the pilot air adjuster home in a clockwise direction. Place gear lever in neutral. Slightly flood the float chamber by gently depressing the tickler until fuel can be seen overflowing from the mixing chamber. Set the magneto at half advance, the throttle approximately one-eighth open, close the air lever and start the engine and warm up.

After warming up, reduce the engine revolutions by gently closing the throttle. The slow-running mixture will prove too rich, unless it happens that air leaks are present. Very gradually unscrew the pilot air adjuster. This will cause the engine speed to increase and it must again be reduced by gently closing the throttle until, by a combination of throttle positions and air adjustment, the desired " idling " is obtained. It is sometimes necessary to retard fully the magneto before good " idling " can be secured, this being particularly so when the magneto runs at engine speed, or when excessive valve overlap and very early ignition timing is employed.

If the desire is that the engine should continue to " idle " with the throttle lever closed, the position of the throttle valve must be set by means of the throttle stop screw, the throttle lever being in the closed position during the adjustment. Alternatively, the screw may be adjusted clear of the throttle valve, in which case the engine will shut off in the normal way by the control lever. On no account should the throttle stop screw (TS, Fig. 16) be taken out completely.

Failure to " idle " may be due to faulty inlet valve and exhaust valve seatings; sparking plug gap too small; sparking plug in an oily state; ignition too much advanced; dirty contacts or contacts set too close on the magneto; oily slip ring; carbon brush jammed in its holder or glazed on the contact face; high-tension cables shorting; or the magneto insulation may be broken down or the interior mechanism may be wet.

3. *The Throttle Valve Cut-away.* If the " idling " speed is satisfactory, set the magneto control at half-advance with the air lever fully open. Then very slowly open the throttle valve when, if the engine responds regularly up to one-quarter throttle, the valve cut-away is correct.

A weak mixture is recognized by spitting back through the air intake with blue flames, and hesitation in picking up (this disappears when the air lever is closed down). Fitting a throttle valve with less cut-away is the remedy.

CARBURATION

Black smoke from the exhaust indicates a rich mixture. The engine stops, or nearly stops, when the air valve is closed. The remedy for this is a throttle valve with more cut-away.

The Amal carburettor fitted to the Triumph is stamped with two numbers, the first indicating the Type No. of the carburettor, and the second the amount of cut-away on the intake side of the valve in sixteenths of an inch. Thus, 6/4 is a Type 6 Valve with $\frac{4}{16}$ in. or $\frac{1}{4}$ in. cut-away. The standard valve for single-cylinder engines is No. 5, and for multi-cylinder engines, No. 4.

4. *Needle Position.* Needle positions are counted from the top of the needle, so the groove nearest the needle top is No. 1. With air full open, open the throttle half-way, and note if the exhaust is crisp and the engine lively. Close the air valve slightly below throttle when the exhaust note and engine speed should remain practically unaltered. Raise the needle in the throttle valve, if popping back and spitting occur with blue flames from the carburettor intake; test by lowering the air valve gently, and note whether the engine revolutions rise when the air valve is lowered slightly below the throttle valve, as they should. Lower the needle in the throttle valve, if the engine speed does not increase progressively as the throttle is raised, if the exhaust is smoky and the running laboured, and if there is a tendency to missfire and eight-stroke on closing the air valve slightly below the throttle valve. The normal needle setting is with the needle clip in No. 3 groove.

When the correct needle position has been found, the carburettor setting is complete, and driving will be practically automatic when once the engine has been warmed up.

Where extreme economy is desired the needle should be lowered one groove further after carrying out the range of tests, as above.

For speed work the main jet may be increased by 10 per cent, when the air lever should be fully opened when on full throttle.

The Carburettor on the 1946 and new Triumph Models. An Amal carburettor is also used on the 1946-9 Triumph models. The settings have been determined after careful experiment and, unless for some special purpose, an improvement in results is unlikely by any different setting. There are a few points in connexion with the upkeep of this component which may be mentioned here. The carburettor should always be kept clean, particularly during the running-in period when the motor-cycle is new. In fact, it is advisable to dismantle it completely for cleaning purposes two or three times during the first 1200 miles running. The joint washer between the carburettor flange and the cylinder head, or induction pipe, should be inspected to see that it is in good condition and not leaking. When the engine is decarbonized it is always a wise plan to fit a new washer. On the 500 c.c. models the joints between the induction pipe and the two inlet ports should be examined when the engine is decarbonized, not only to see if they are in good condition, but not overlapping the bore. If new gaskets are fitted a gasket cement should be used on the cylinder head flange. All nuts must be tightened up a little at a time, alternately, or such strain may be imposed on the flange that it fractures.

Because of the correct proportions of the jet sizes and the main choke bore, the carburettor proportions and atomizes the right amount of petrol with the air that is induced into the engine. A constant level is maintained by the float chamber at the jets, and the supply is cut off when the engine is stopped. The volume of mixture is controlled by the throttle control on the handlebar, and the mixture is automatically correct at all throttle openings. When the throttle is opened it brings into action the mixture supply from the pilot jet system for idling; as it is progressively opened the mixture is augmented from the main jet, the earlier stages of which action are controlled by the needle in the needle jet. The main jet discharges through the needle jet into the primary air chamber—not directly into the mixing chamber—and goes thence as a rich petrol-air mixture through the primary choke bore into the main air choke; this primary air choke has a compensating action. The carburettor has a specially operated mixture control called an air valve for use when starting from cold, as mentioned in a previous chapter.

It is suggested in Chapter X ("Faults and their Diagnosis"), that it is usually advisable when the engine fails to start, runs irregularly or stops to examine the carburation system first, as the trouble may lie with the carburettor. If, however, the trouble cannot be remedied by making the mixture weaker or richer by means of the air valve, and it is known that the fuel feed is in order and that the carburettor is not flooding, the cause of the trouble lies elsewhere. Weakness or richness of the mixture are the only two faults in carburation. To determine whether it is weakness or richness: 1. Examine the petrol supply, verifying that the jets and passages are clear, the flow ample and that there is no flooding. 2. Look for air leaks at the connexion to the engine or owing to leaky inlet valve stems. 3. Inspect for worn or defective parts, such as a slack throttle, worn needle jet, loose jets or the union nut of the mixing chamber is not fully tightened. 4. Test by means of the air valve to ascertain whether by enriching the mixture better or worse results are obtained.

Weakness is indicated by; Spitting in the carburettor, erratic slow running, overheating, poor acceleration; richness by black

CARBURATION

smoke in the exhaust, fuel spraying out the carburettor, eight-stroking, heavy lumpy running, heavy petrol consumption. Further, if the air valve is partially closed at a particular throttle opening, and the engine runs better, weakness is suggested; if the running is not so good, richness is indicated. Then adjust the appropriate part as indicated by Fig. 17.

To cure weakness: 1. Fit a larger main jet. 2. Screw pilot air screw in. 3. Fit a throttle with smaller cut-away. 4. Raise

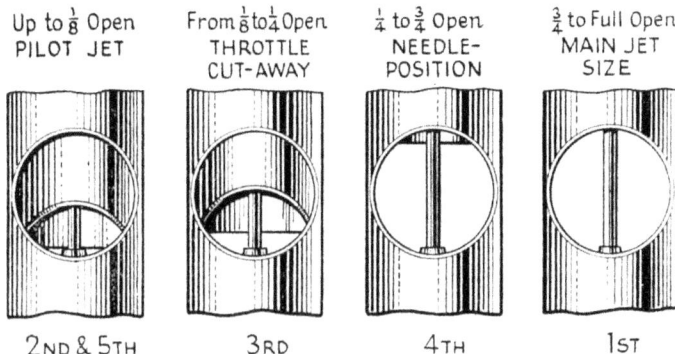

Fig. 17. Phases of Amal Needle Jet Carburettor Throttle Openings

needle one or two grooves. To cure richness: 1. Fit a smaller main jet. 2. Screw out pilot air screw. 3. Fit a throttle with larger cut-away. 4. Lower needle one or two grooves. It should be noted that it is not correct procedure when curing a rich mixture at half throttle to fit a smaller main jet, because this jet may be correct for power at full throttle; lowering the needle is the right thing to do.

Re-assembling after Dismantling. The principal points to notice when re-assembling is that the mixing chamber nut E (Fig. 15) is tight on the washer that holds the jet block F (Fig. 15); if not properly tightened petrol will leak up. When the throttle is being replaced it is important to see that the throttle needle goes into the centre hole in the choke block and, once in, that the throttle works freely when the mixing chamber top ring is screwed down firmly and held by the spring.

CHAPTER IV

LUBRICATION: ROUTINE TASKS AND MAINTENANCE HINTS

THE oil film between the several contacting surfaces of the working parts of a motor-cycle is equal in importance to the quality of the materials used in making the various components of the machine. Adequate and proper lubrication means supplying a sufficient quantity of the right kind of oil or grease. If the quantity of lubricant is sufficient but the quality is low and the grade incorrect, or, on the other hand, if the quality and grade are correct but the supply deficient, trouble is certain to be encountered and the serviceable life of the motor-cycle reduced.

ENGINE LUBRICATION

The engine operates at a high speed and this is conducive to comparatively high temperatures, so it is imperative that only oils of the best and proved quality be used. Lubricant in constant circulation collects many substances, such as unburnt fuel, moisture through condensation, carbon, and gritty and metallic particles of an abrasive nature; these all create wear and should be extracted without delay. The selection of the oil is in the hands of the motor-cyclist, and it is also his duty to look after the system.

Recommended Lubricants. Reference to Figs. 18 and 19 will assist the Triumph owner to choose the correct lubricant, as these indicate the brands and grades recommended by the factory.

Dry Sump System (1935-6). The system on all 1935-6 Triumph models is of the dry sump type. Circulation is carried out by means of a double plunger pump driven by the exhaust camshaft with predetermined velocity, so no adjustment is necessary. Model 6/1, the 650 c.c. Vertical Twin, has a single plunger taking impulse from the camshaft.

On all 1935-6 Triumph models, with the exception of 6/1, the oil is carried in a separate tank, where it is drawn through a filter, the flow commencing as engine movement begins, by the smaller pump plunger through pressure valves, where the duct is tapped for indication at the tank button (except L2/1), along the gear shaft, with determined release for time gear and magneto drive, to the big-end bearing, where small clearances allow escape, efficiently to lubricate, by slinging, the cylinder walls, piston, gudgeon-pin bearing and mainshaft bearing; the surplus drains through the filter to the sump for withdrawal to the tank by means of the second plunger.

No tap is included in the system, for the oil circuit is automatically closed when the engine ceases to move.

On Model 6/1 the same principle is employed, but it differs in its application. The single plunger pump—return is by gravity to the sump in the base—is housed at the bottom of the engine; oil is passed to the pressure tank (tapped for indication) through the filter, via the release valve to the crankshaft bearing and timing gear, and is subsequently distributed by the splash method.

On Model 5/10 an adjustable feed to the rear of the cylinder is controlled by a needle valve on the off-side.

On Models L2/1, 2/1 and 3/2 the overhead valve gear lubrication is automatic with adjustable flow; on other models the rocker spindle, and in some cases the valve guide lubrication is by grease nipple. The grease gun should be used every 250 miles, and the recommended lubricants are Castrolease Medium Shell Retinax, Price's Belmoline C, Essogrease, and Mobilgrease No. 2. On models which have exposed valve springs the frequent application of a little engine oil to the stems is advantageous.

Dry Sump System (1937-9 Models). All 1937-9 models are fitted with dry sump lubrication similar in general design and principle to the 1935-6 system just dealt with. However, there are differences, and to avoid any confusion a full description of the 1937-9 system will be given.

The engine oil is fed from the oil tank beneath the saddle through a pipe to the pressure side of the oil pump (Fig. 20). The pump then forces the oil through the drilled crankshaft assembly to the big-end(s) where it emerges in the form of mist which thoroughly lubricates the internal components of the power unit.

On 1937-9 single- and 1939 twin-cylinder Triumph engines the oil pressure is regulated by means of a release valve situated at the back of the timing case or in the centre of the timing case respectively. The release valve comprises a ball which is normally held on its seat by means of a coil spring. When, however, the pressure of the oil rises above normal (see page 43), the ball is raised off its seat and permits surplus oil to flow to the bottom of the crankcase. Thus the pressure of the release valve spring automatically determines the oil pressure, assuming that the oil is circulating properly. Oil after circulating through the engine falls to the bottom of the crankcase through a large gauze filter, and is then picked up by the suction side of the oil pump and forced back into the oil tank.

Unit	B.P.	Wakefield	Esso	Vacuum	Shell
Engine {Summer {Winter	Energol SAE 30 Energol SAE 20	Castrol XL Castrolite	Essolube 30 Essolube 20	Mobiloil A Mobiloil Arctic	Shell X-100 30 Shell X-100 20/20W
Gearbox . . .	Energol SAE 30	Castrol XL	Essolube 30	Mobiloil A	Shell X-100 30
Primary Chaincase .	Energol SAE 20	Castrolite	Essolube 20	Mobiloil Arctic	Shell X-100 20/20W
Telescopic Fork .	Energol SAE 20	Castrolite	Essolube 20	Mobiloil Arctic	Shell X-100 20/20W
Spring Wheel Mechanism	Energrease C3G	Castrolease Graphited or Castrolease Heavy	Esso Graphite Grease	Mobil Graphited Grease	Shell Retinax A or RB
Spring Wheel Ball Bearing	Energrease C3	Castrolease Heavy	Esso Grease	Mobilgrease No. 2	Shell Retinax A or RB
Grease Gun and Rocker Gear . .	Energrease C3	Castrolease CL	Esso Grease	Mobilgrease No. 2	Shell Retinax A or RB
Easing Rusted Parts .	Energol Penetrating Oil	Castrol Penetrating Oil	Esso Penetrating Oil	Mobil Spring Oil	Shell Donax P

Fig. 18. Recommended Lubricants for Post-war Models (United Kingdom)

Unit	B.P.	Wakefield	Esso	Vacuum	Shell
Engine { Above 90° F.	Energol SAE 40	Castrol XXL	Esso Motor Oil 40	Mobiloil A.F.	Shell X-100 40
Engine { 32°–90° F.	Energol SAE 30	Castrol XL	Esso Motor Oil 30	Mobiloil A	Shell X-100 30
Engine { Below 32° F.	Energol SAE 20W	Castrolite	Esso Motor Oil 20W	Mobiloil Arctic	Shell X-100 20/20W
Gearbox	Energol SAE 30	Castrol XL	Esso Motor Oil 30	Mobiloil A	Shell X-100 30
Primary Chaincase	Energol SAE 20W	Castrolite	Esso Motor Oil 20W	Mobiloil Arctic	Shell X-100 20/20W
Telescopic Fork	Energol SAE 20W	Castrolite	Esso Motor Oil 20W	Mobiloil Arctic	Shell X-100 20/20W
Spring Wheel Mechanism	Energrease C3G	Castrolease Graphited or Castrolease Heavy	Esso Chassis Grease	Mobil Graphited Grease	Shell Retinax A or B
Spring Wheel Ball Bearing	Energrease C3	Castrolease Heavy	Esso Bearing Grease	Mobilgrease No. 2	Shell Retinax A or B
Grease Gun and Rocker Gear	Energrease C3	Castrolease CL	Esso Bearing Grease	Mobilgrease No. 2	Shell Retinax A or B
Easing Rusted Parts	Energol Penetrating Oil	Castrol Penetrating Oil	Esso Penetrating Oil	Mobil Spring Oil	Shell Donax P

FIG. 18A. RECOMMENDED LUBRICANTS FOR POST-WAR MODELS (OVERSEAS)

Unit	Esso	Wakefield	Shell	Vacuum	BP Energol
Engine	Racer	XXL	X100-50	D	SAE 20
Gearbox	Racer	XXL	X100-50	D	SAE 50
Chain case	20	Castrolite	X100-20/20W	Arctic	SAE 20
Grease Gun and Rocker Gear	Essogrease	Castrolease C.L.	Retinax A	Mobilgrease No. 2	Energrease C3
Easing rusted parts	Esso Penetrating Oil	Castrol Penetrating Oil	Shell Donax P	Mobil Spring Oil	Energol Penetrating Oil

FIG. 19. RECOMMENDED LUBRICANTS FOR PRE-1946 SINGLE-CYLINDER MODELS

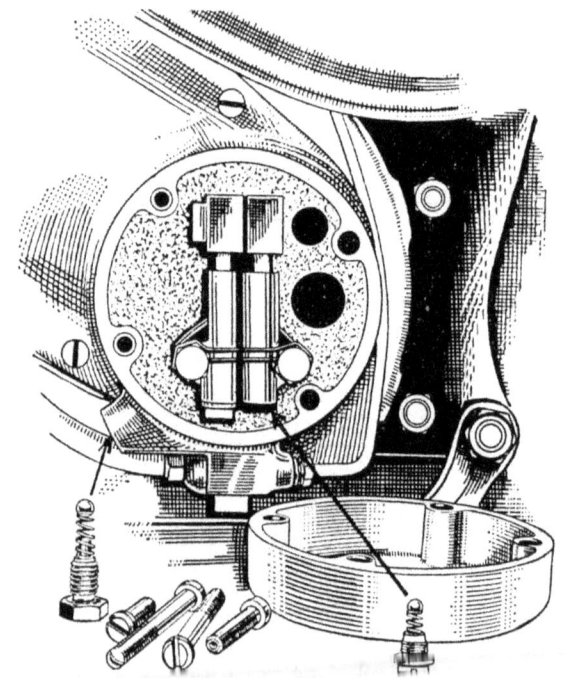

FIG. 20. OIL PUMP ARRANGEMENT (1937–9 SINGLES)
An illustration showing the lay-out on the "Speed Twin" and "Tiger 100" will be found on page 96

The capacity of the suction side of the pump is twice as great as that of the delivery or pressure side, and this ensures that the engine sump remains "dry." The delivery pipe on the O.H.V. models is tapped, a by-pass pipe (external) leading some of the oil direct to the rocker box. The feed to the rocker box is adjustable in the case of single-cylinder engines. On these engines oil after being forced through the rocker shafts collects at the base of the rocker box and by means of oil return pipes is returned to the crankcase. Oil from the rocker box on twin-cylinder engines is conveyed by pipes to the upper ends of the push rod tubes and is returned by gravity to the crankcase after lubricating the cams and tappet gear. An extension of the pipe to the rocker box on O.H.V. engines is connected to the oil pressure gauge on the instrument panel.

Engine Lubrication (1946 Models). The lubrication of the 1946 Triumphs may be dealt with in some detail. Dry sump lubrication is adopted. The oil is contained in a tank fitted under the saddle, and it is fed through a pipe to the pressure side of the

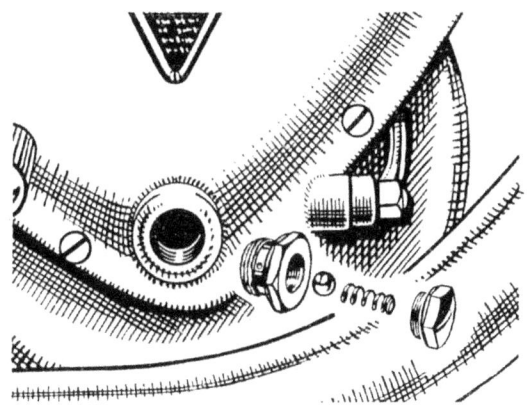

FIG. 21. SHOWING OIL PRESSURE RELEASE VALVE (1939 TWINS)
On the 1937-9 singles the release valve is situated at the back of the timing case as shown in Fig. 20

oil pump. Thence it is forced through the crankshaft assembly, which is drilled for the purpose, and issues from the big-ends in the form of an oil fog which serves to lubricate the internal parts of the engine. A release valve regulates the pressure, this being located in the centre of the timing cover on the Tiger "100" and the Speed Twin, and the front offside crankcase on the 3T de Luxe. The valve consists of a piston and spring and, in the event of the oil pressure becoming excessive, the piston is forced back on its spring, allowing surplus oil to pass through the uncovered hole in the release valve body to the crankcase. The strength of the oil pressure release valve spring regulates the poundage of the oil pressure.

The oil falls to the bottom of the crankcase through the filter, after lubricating the engine, whence it is picked up by the suction side of the oil pump and returned to the oil tank. In order to make certain that no liquid oil remains on the floor of the crankcase,

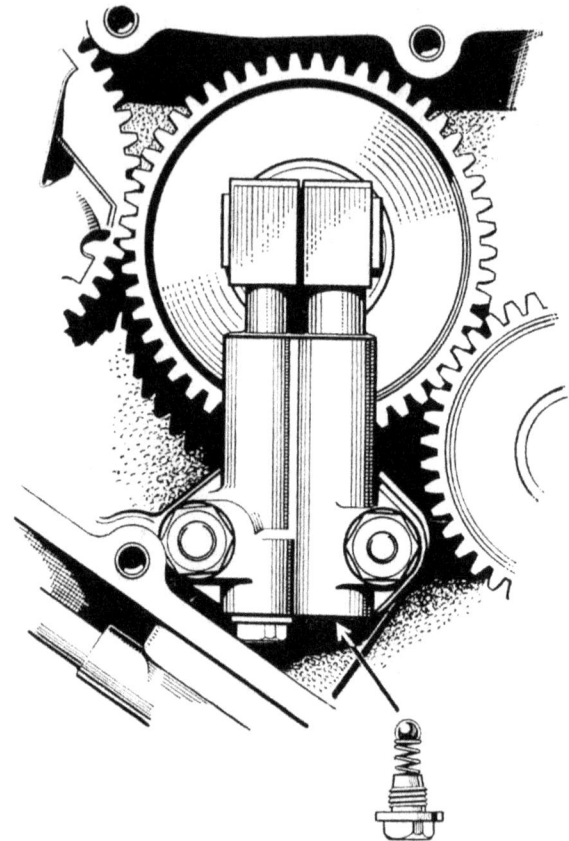

FIG. 22. OIL PUMP ON 1946 MODELS

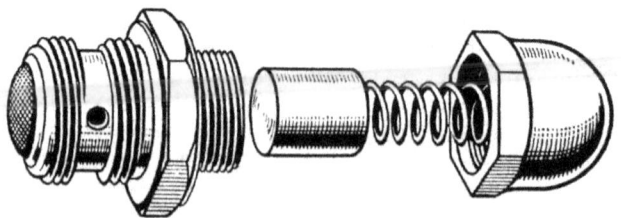

FIG. 23. OIL PRESSURE RELEASE VALVE

the suction side of the oil pump has twice the capacity of the pressure side. The O.H.V. rocker gear is supplied with oil taken from the return oil scavenge pipe by tapping it just below the oil

LUBRICATION

tank. After being forced through the rocker shafts the oil drains down the oil return holes in the cylinder block and down the push rod tubes to the bottom of the crankcase after lubricating the cams and tappets. On the 350 c.c. twin the oil drains to the crankcase through the push rod tubes only.

Mounted on the instrument panel the oil pressure gauge registers the pressure at which the system is working. As mentioned previously, the minimum running oil pressure should be 35 lb. per square inch when the engine is hot and the machine running on the road. When the oil is cold and thick, as it is in winter, the pressure registered is high; the reading falls as the oil attains its normal working temperature.

Reference is made in Chapter I to the lubrication improvements introduced on post-war standard models.

Changing the Engine Oil

Engine Lubrication (1935-6 Models). The oil level should be checked constantly—in the tank, excepting in the case of Model 6/1—and topped up, if materially below the bottom of the filler tube or half an inch of "High" mark respectively.

The system should be drained for the first time after preliminary running-in—at 750 miles. Afterwards it is sufficient at 1500-mile intervals. Remove the filter boss or drain plug from the tank and the base plate, or plug (6/1) from sump, the best time for draining being on the completion of a run when the heated conditions allow the oil to flow freely, so any impurity therein is cleared out more effectively.

Filtering units are integral with the crankcase base plate or plug on all engines, and with disk in oil and pressure (6/1) tanks to which the oil feed pipe is attached. All these are easily detachable and should be cleaned by washing in paraffin. It should be noted that all cloth used in connexion with any part of the lubrication system should be of a non-fluffy nature.

The system should not be flushed with paraffin, since this tends to loosen, but not remove, deposits which are better left untouched until the engine is dismantled for overhaul. Great care should be taken to avoid stressing threads of adaptors and bolts, although satisfactory joints naturally depend on even security.

Engine Lubrication (1937-9 Models). About every 250 miles remove the filler cap of the oil tank, inspect the oil level and, if necessary, top up with suitable engine oil. The tank should preferably be kept filled to within 2 in. of the filler orifice, that is just below the opening of the return pipe. On no account must the level of oil be allowed to fall below the minimum level mark. During the running-in period to prevent oil contamination the oil should be changed at intervals of 250, 500, and 1000 miles. Subsequently it should be sufficient to change the oil once every 1500 miles. Do this after a run when the engine oil is warm. When changing the oil the tank should be flushed out with flushing oil (obtainable from most garages and accessory dealers). It is not necessary to discard the flushing oil after use as this may be filtered through a piece of muslin and used again. It is also important when changing the oil to remove and clean the filters. Two filters are provided, one in the oil tank and one in the crankcase. On 1939 twin-cylinder models there is an additional filter

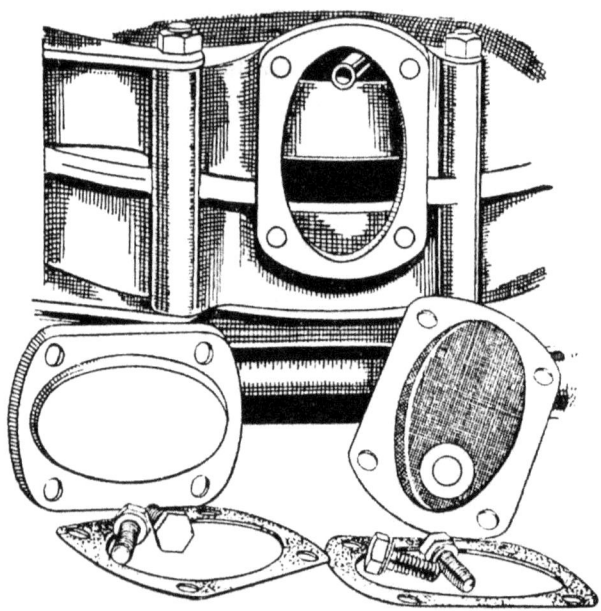

FIG. 24. BOTTOM OF CRANKCASE SHOWING FILTER DETACHED

incorporated in the oil pressure release valve body on the timing case.

To remove the tank filter on single-cylinder engines, remove the oil pipe block beneath the timing case and disconnect the two feed pipes by withdrawing them from their rubber connecting tubes. Then unscrew the large hexagonal nut on the tank and remove this together with the filter. In the case of the twin-cylinder engines do not remove the oil pipe block, because there is a readily detachable oil pipe joint. To remove the crankcase filter (Fig. 24), undo the four hexagonal headed screws which secure the filter to the crankcase and remove the baseplate and filter. Removal of the filter in the pressure release valve on the 1939 twin-cylinder models is merely a question of unscrewing the body from the timing case. Having removed the filters, wash them thoroughly in petrol and avoid using a fluffy rag on the gauze. When replacing the crankcase filter, see that the washers are undamaged and clean and tighten the screws evenly. After completing the operation of draining the tank, flushing out, replenishment and cleaning of the filters, go over the various unions and the tank drain plug with a spanner so as to verify that they are absolutely tight before attempting to start up. As soon as the engine starts, check the oil pressure at the gauge on the instrument panel and also remove the tank filler cap and note if the oil is being returned.

A close watch should at all times be kept on the oil circulation and pressure. On the single-cylinder models if oil is observed issuing from the return pipe, the lubrication system *must* be functioning satisfactorily, but on the twin-cylinder models the fact that oil is returning to the tank is not definite proof that sufficient oil is passing through the crankshaft assembly and lubricating the engine. A minimum oil pressure of 35 lb. per sq. in. *must* also be recorded by the pressure gauge. On the singles the minimum safe pressure is 5 lb. per sq. in. Stop the engine *at once* if pressure fluctuates or falls below the minimum safe reading. On overhead-valve engines the oil pressure is indicated within a few moments of starting up, but in the case of side-valve engines the pressure may take some time to build up. In cold weather high initial readings are normal, but these quickly settle down to the correct reading. Complete absence of oil pressure or a very low pressure may be caused by the ball in the oil pressure release valve being held off its seating by some foreign particle. Rarely, however, does this trouble arise. As a safeguard the valve on the 1939 twin-cylinder engines is protected by a gauze filter. A fall in oil pressure is seldom due to the gauge itself being out of order as this is extremely reliable. It may generally be rectified by dismantling and cleaning the pressure release valve and giving the ball (Fig. 21) a sharp tap on its seating before replacing it. Do not interfere with the piston type valve situated in the timing cover on 1938 twin-cylinder engines.

With the Triumph design of oil pump all parts are constantly immersed in oil, and wear, therefore, takes place very slowly. Hence do not immediately suspect the pump when some lubrication trouble arises. It is very unlikely to be responsible. The only part likely to wear after a very considerable mileage is the pump drive block which may be replaced for a small sum.

As has been referred to previously, the suction side of the pump is of greater capacity than the delivery side. For this reason the return of oil to the tank on all models is intermittent and the presence of some air bubbles is to be expected. The normal condition is for a spurt of oil to be seen for a few moments, followed by a few air bubbles. Failure of the oil to return to the tank results in the crankcase filling up, which causes bad smoking and oil to be blown out of the breather. Incomplete scavenging of the crankcase by the return oil pump is generally due to a choked air vent on top of the oil tank. This vent maintains atmospheric pressure in the tank and is connected to the frame by a rubber tube so as to lead away obnoxious fumes. Any obstruction of the vent or kinking of the rubber tube causes pressure to be built up inside the tank with the result that proper crankcase scavenging does not occur. The remedy for this trouble is obvious.

A possible cause of the Triumph pump not working satisfactorily is imperfect seating of the two spring-loaded ball valves at the foot of the pump (Fig. 20). To rectify the trouble, remove the balls and clean them and their seats thoroughly. In extreme instances it may be desirable to remove the pump body from the engine, and sharply tap the balls on to their seats before reassembling. When replacing the oil pump cover, see that the joint washer is absolutely clean and intact; also be sure to retighten the four cover screws evenly and firmly.

Engine Lubrication (1946 Models). The oil should be changed frequently during the running-in period, so as to make certain that any foreign matter picked up by the oil in the course of circulation shall be removed. It is advisable to change the oil at 250, 500, and 1000 miles during this initial period, and afterwards every 1500 miles. The filters should be cleaned when the oil is changed. The filter in the oil tank is removed by breaking the union under the oil tank and unscrewing the large hexagonal nut to which the filter is fitted. Four hexagonal-headed screws under the crankcase secure the crankcase filter. To dismantle the filter these must be removed. The oil pressure release valve (Fig. 23) should also be removed to facilitate cleaning the filter in the release valve body. The best way to clean these filters is by washing in petrol. The oil tank should be flushed out with a flushing oil (obtainable from most garages and accessory dealers). When the system has been drained and refilled all joints and the drain plug should be tightened up before the engine is started. As soon as the engine has been started up, check the oil pressure, and see that the oil is returning to the tank.

The oil tank should be filled to within two inches of the filler. The oil pressure should never fall below 35 lb. per square inch with the machine on the road; stop the engine if this pressure is not being registered, as failure to do so may result in serious damage. The fact that oil is returning to the tank is not proof

LUBRICATION

that the system is working correctly. The return of oil to the oil tank is intermittent; a spurt of oil for a few moments, then a few air bubbles. This is because the suction side of the oil pump has double the capacity of the pressure side. It may happen on occasion that the oil does not return properly to the tank, with the result that the crankcase fills up and the engine smokes and, probably oil blows out of the breather. Should these symptoms

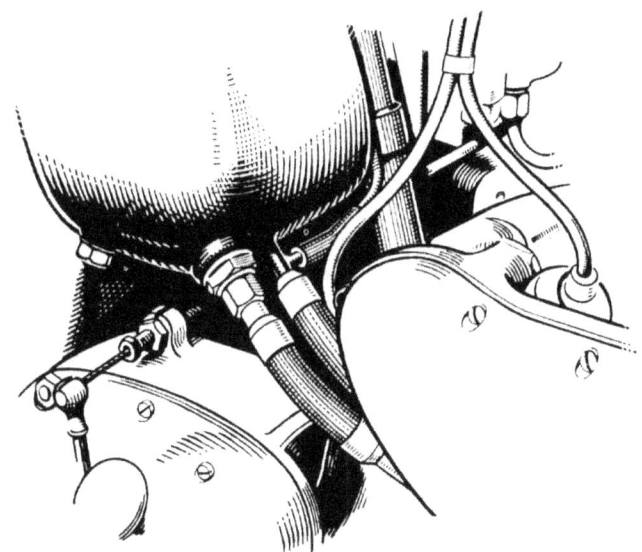

Fig. 25. Oil Tank (1946 Models)
Showing drain plug and oil pipe union. After union nut has been disconnected the oil filter can be screwed out

arise examine the vent at the top of the oil tank, as it may be obstructed; clear, if necessary. Or, the tube connecting the vent to the frame may be kinked, in which case pressure builds up in the oil tank and prevents a proper scavenge of the crankcase.

The pump will not function in a satisfactory manner if the balls underneath the oil pump are seating badly; remove the balls for cleaning, but in extreme cases it may be necessary to remove the pump body, when the balls can be given a sharp tap on their seatings.

If the oil pressure gauge registers nil, or a very low pressure, the cause may be that the piston in the oil pressure release valve is held above the bleed hole by foreign matter. The valve is protected by a filter gauze, so this trouble is not liable to occur. Should the pressure fall dismantle the valve for cleaning and examine the piston for freeness in the valve body. The oil pressure gauge is a very reliable unit; lack of oil pressure is seldom due to a fault in it.

Lubrication of Overhead Valve Gear (1937-9 Models). Single-cylinder and twin-cylinder models employ force feed lubrication of the rocker box, the oil being conveyed by an external pipe. As in the case of some 1935-6 models, the oil feed to the rocker box on all single-cylinder engines may be adjusted if desired by means of a hexagon-headed screw and locknut situated at the front of the rocker box on the off-side. To increase the oil supply to the overhead rockers and valve guides, screw the adjuster screw *out* and to reduce the supply, screw the adjuster screw in. To verify how much oil is actually being fed to the overhead valve gear, slacken off the two plated acorn nuts on the banjo unions to the rocker spindles and ease the feed pipe away from the rocker box with a screwdriver. Then start up the engine and note how much oil is leaking from the banjo unions. This oil normally passes through the rocker spindles, and therefore indicates the amount of oil supplied to the overhead valve gear. If the adjustment is correct, there should only be a slight trickle of oil when testing in the above manner. Do not adjust so as to give an excessive oil supply, otherwise oil leakage is inevitable.

On twin-cylinder engines there is no means of adjusting the oil supply to the rocker box. Fitted into the rocker box oil pipe near the timing case is a threaded restrictor plug and oil forces its way between the threads of this plug and the body into which it fits, in the correct amount to lubricate properly the overhead valve gear. If it is desired to find out how much oil is being supplied, test in the same way as described for the single-cylinder engines. In the unlikely event of the oil supply being insufficient, it is possible to increase the supply by removing the restrictor plug and running a die down the threads.

Lubrication of Overhead Valve Gear (1946 and 1949 Models). The rocker feed pipe requires no adjustment; the supply is taken direct from the oil scavenge pipe underneath the oil tank. When the engine is running the oil passes through the rocker shafts to lubricate the parts. The supply can be checked by slackening the two acorn nuts on the banjo unions to the rocker spindles, and the pipe assembly eased away from the rocker box by means of a screwdriver.

GEAR-BOX

After every 1000 miles running the oil level should be brought up to that of the level plug, except in the case of 6/1, where the correct level allows the oil just to show in the base of the filling well.

On 1937-9 models the level plug is situated at the back of the kick-starter casing underneath the tool-box. Care should be taken **never** to over-fill the gear-box and in no circumstances should thick

LUBRICATION

gear oil be used for replenishment. Before topping up the gear-box always make sure that the level plug is first removed, otherwise excessive lubricant will enter the box and cause leakage and heavy gear changing. All Triumph gear-boxes are designed to operate with engine oil as the lubricant. Suitable brands and grades of engine oil are: Patent Castrol XXL, Golden Shell (Extra Heavy), Mobiloil D, Price's C De Luxe, and Essolube Racer. About every 5000 miles the drain plug should be removed and the gear-box completely drained, flushed out and replenished with fresh oil. The drain plug will be found at the back of the gear-box. In the case of a brand new machine it is advisable to drain and refill the gear-box after the first 500 miles and subsequently at intervals of 5000 miles. A broken open view of the new Triumph gear-box provided on 1946 models will be found on page 95.

The grease gun should be applied (1935–6 boxes) to the nipple on the clutch lever greasing thrust ball, and to the nipple on the hand lever fulcrum bolt or the foot control body. The oilcan should be used on the ball ends of the gear rod, the clutch cable nipple housing, and the engaging faces of the hand lever and quadrant should be kept covered with a film of oil or grease. The clutch push rod should be withdrawn now and again, the cable being detached from the lever to allow egress, and well greased.

The gear-box of the 1946–9 Triumphs should be lubricated with engine oil; a thick gear oil must not be used in any circumstance. The filler plug is located on the gear-box cover, and the drain plug at the back of the box. The level plug is in the rear portion of the gear-box inner cover below the tool-box. An excessive quantity of oil should not be put into the gear-box, as this makes for a very hard change.

PRIMARY CHAINCASE AND REAR CHAIN

Chains. On those models on which primary drive oil bath cases are fitted inspect occasionally and keep the oil up to the level plug; this part should be drained every 1000 miles, using the base plug. The vent in the filler plug must be kept clear.

Models having chain covers have a positive oil feed to the primary chain, and the flow is readily adjustable (see Fig. 26), as this supply is taken from the main engine oil line; the pressure requires only a slight opening on the regulator. The nozzle of the pipe should be properly directed adjacent to the chain links. Rear chain lubrication is automatic on all models, by crankcase ventilation breathing through a pipe to a point near the gear-box sprocket on 1935–8 models. On these models it is important to keep the release clear. It is unlikely that trouble will be experienced, but should the secondary chain be noticed running dry, it will be necessary to detach the primary oil-bath chaincase and remove and clean the oil pipe and disc valve on the crankcase. Do this with petrol. No adjustment of the release valve is ever needed.

On 1939 models the secondary chain is lubricated by an adjustable lubricator situated at the rear of the primary chain case. Lubricating oil from the chain case is fed by splash into a small receptacle, and from here it is supplied to the secondary chain in an amount determined by the adjustment of the regulator screw. The screw should be adjusted so that the chain receives just sufficient lubrication. To commence with, unscrew the

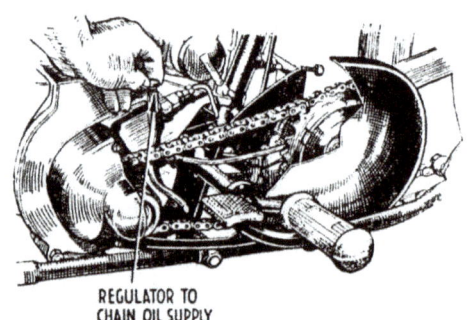

Fig. 26. 1935–6 Primary Chain Adjustable Oil Feed

regulator 2½ turns from the right in position. About every 1000 miles in summer and every 1500 miles in winter the secondary chain should be removed, immersed in a bath of paraffin and dried. It should then be submerged in a bath of graphite grease and oil heated over a tin of boiling water. See that the grease penetrates into all the chain bearings before refitting the chain. When refitting on the sprockets, make sure that the spring link has the open end facing *away from* the direction of motion.

With the 1946–9 Triumphs the clutch, primary chain, engine shock absorber and engine sprocket are situated inside the primary chaincase. Lubrication is by means of a special thin oil poured into the case through the filler plug. Only the correct grade should be used; the right quantity is half a pint. The drain plug is underneath the case. Every time the two halves of the case are separated, a new paper washer should be used; jointing compound should not be employed on the faces of the primary chaincase.

At the rear of the primary chaincase is an adjustable lubricator by means of which the rear chain is lubricated. Oil from the chaincase is fed by splash into a small receptacle, whence it is delivered to the rear chain in a quantity which is governed by the adjustment of a screw.

LUBRICATION 49

BICYCLE PARTS

All components provided with grease nipples for lubricating purposes should be attended to at regular intervals. The lubricants recommended for use in the grease gun are given in Figs.

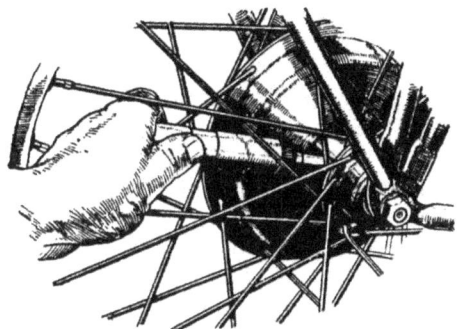

FIG. 27. HOW THE OIL-GUN IS USED

18 and 19. If a heavier grade is used, the various bearings and bushes may be starved with consequent rapid wear. The manner in which the oil gun is used is shown in Fig. 27.

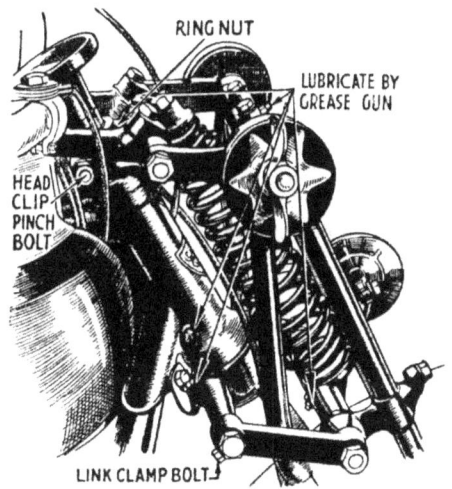

FIG. 28. SHOWING STEERING LUBRICATION POINTS

Steering. The grease gun should be used every 1000 miles on the steering head and fork spindles; there are five points in all (Fig. 28). Do not over lubricate the centre-fork bridge, otherwise grease may get on the friction dampers.

1935-7 Twist-grip and Controls. Apply grease at regular intervals to the internal mechanism of the twist-grip by releasing the fixing end clip (Fig. 1), allowing this and the inverted lever plug to be withdrawn sufficiently to disclose the slides to which grease should be lightly applied. Cable nipple housings, fulcrum pins, etc., should be oiled. Do not forget the saddle and rear stand fulcrum pins.

Wheels. The grease gun should be applied every 1000 miles to the nipples of the wheel hubs if the machine is a 1935-9 model; the hubs should be repacked with grease every 10,000 miles if the mount is a 1946 model. Besides greasing the only attention likely to be called for is an occasional adjustment of the hub bearings; this is discussed in Chapter VI. The introduction of a spring wheel in the 3T de Luxe, Speed Twin, and Tiger "100" standard models, and the "Trophy" and "Grand Prix" 1949 models, is an event of outstanding interest. The several parts are described and illustrated in Chapter VI, but it may be mentioned here that this wheel has been designed to give a very great mileage before overhaul. A grease nipple is fitted into the off-side of the rear spindle; recommended grease should be pumped through this nipple every 1000 miles.

Controls. At intervals the control cables should be lubricated; stiffness in operation results if they become dry. A good plan is to remove the Bowden wire connexion from the lever at its top and make a funnel with brown paper round the casing, fastening it with a rubber band. If thin machine oil is fed into the funnel, and allowed to remain overnight, it will trickle down the casing and lubricate the cable. Keep the control cables clear of the engine; if they become over-heated the lubricant dries up.

The Triumph twist-grip throttle control is not likely to require any attention.

All brake rod joints and pins should be lubricated by means of the oil can.

Oil Leakage. If properly serviced Triumph motor-cycles do not suffer from oil leakage. Leakage is invariably due to carelessly made joints when the engine is re-assembled.

CHAPTER V

LIGHTING AND ELECTRICAL FITTINGS

THE 1935-9 models except 2HC, 3SC have 6-volt Lucas Magdyno lighting and electric horn. The Magdyno, as its name suggests, consists of two units—a magneto for ignition and a dynamo for charging the battery (Fig. 29). The dynamo unit is detachable, an excellent arrangement when the machine is required for racing or for competition work and the lighting equipment is not needed. A suitable fitment can be obtained for protecting the gears when it is desired to run the mount without the dynamo unit.

Some 1935-6 models are fitted with a headlamp which incorporates the control switch and ammeter, while others have a headlamp with an instrument panel which houses the switch and ammeter, together with the oil gauge (1937-9), and panel light.

On the 1938-9 Models 2HC, 3HC Lucas coil ignition equipment is provided, the dynamo with contact breaker on the near-side taking the place of the Magdyno. Automatic voltage control is included on all 1937-9 models, including those with coil ignition.

The Dynamo. The dynamo on all of the 1935-6 models is fitted with two main brushes; the positive is insulated and the negative is earthed. A third brush is provided on the underside of the commutator bracket and this controls the output of the dynamo by what is known as the third brush method. The object of the third brush system is to regulate the output at high speeds and keep it steady, independent of the speed at which the dynamo is running, for naturally dynamo speed varies with engine speed.

The Cut-out. The cut-out, on the dynamo end bracket (1935-6), is an automatic switch which prevents discharge of the battery when the dynamo is not working. Its contacts close when the dynamo voltage rises above that of the battery as the engine is speeded up, and open when the speed drops and the voltage falls below that of the battery, but it does not prevent overcharging. The cut-out is accurately set before the motor-cycle leaves the works and it should not be adjusted or disturbed.

Automatic Voltage Control. Where automatic voltage control is provided (1937 onwards), the cut-out and regulator are combined as a unit separate from the dynamo. The regulator which is connected across the dynamo brushes dispenses with the "third brush" and operates on the "trembler" principle, automatically

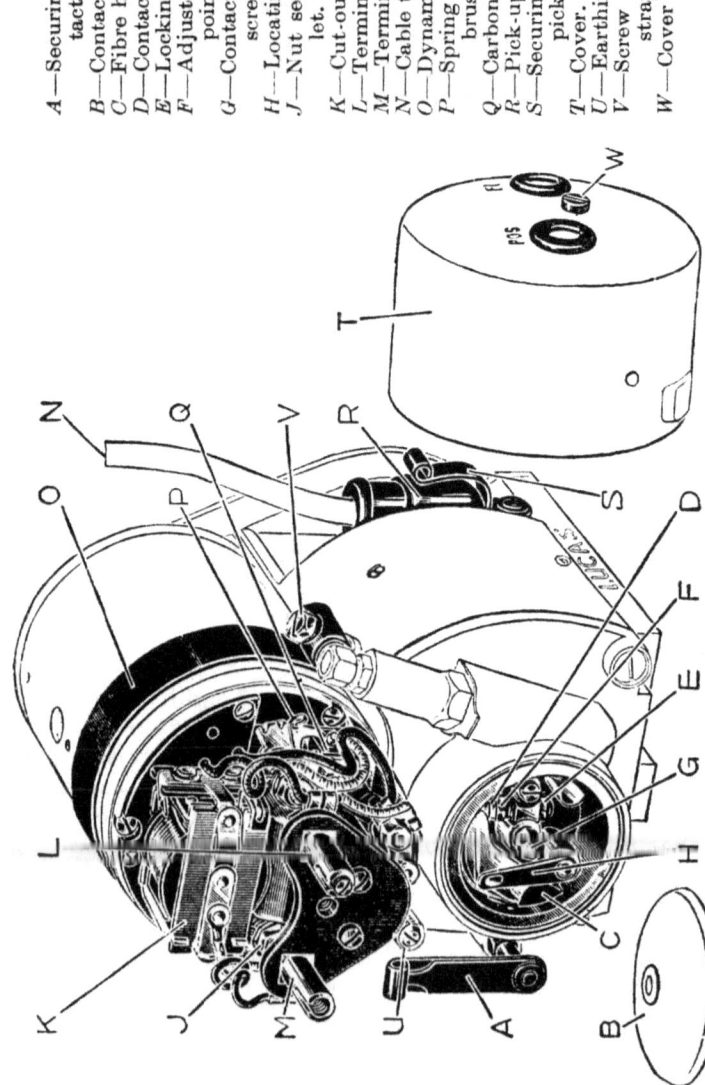

A—Securing spring for contact breaker cover.
B—Contact breaker cover.
C—Fibre heel.
D—Contact points.
E—Locking nut.
F—Adjustable contact point.
G—Contact breaker fixing screw.
H—Locating spring.
J—Nut securing brush eyelet.
K—Cut-out.
L—Terminal marked "F1."
M—Terminal marked "Pos."
N—Cable to sparking plug.
O—Dynamo securing strap.
P—Spring lever holding brush in position.
Q—Carbon brush.
R—Pick-up.
S—Securing spring for pick-up.
T—Cover.
U—Earthing terminal.
V—Screw securing dynamo strap.
W—Cover fixing screw.

Fig. 29. View of 1935-6 Lucas "Magdyno" with Cut-out

LIGHTING AND ELECTRICAL FITTINGS

varying the output of the dynamo according to the state of charge of the battery and the load. Thus charging is purely automatic and not under the control of the rider, as in the case where automatic voltage control is not fitted (1935-6).

The Headlamp. The headlamp is fitted with a double-filament bulb; one filament is arranged to be approximately at the focus of the reflector and gives the normal driving light, while the second one, mounted slightly above the other, gives a dipped, anti-dazzling beam for use when meeting traffic or driving in mist or fog, this device being controlled by a switch mounted on the handlebars. A small pilot bulb is also provided for use when the machine is stationary, and for town riding.

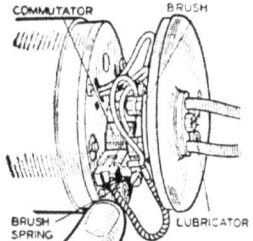

FIG. 30. COMMUTATOR END OF 1937-9 LUCAS DYNAMO WITH SEPARATE AUTOMATIC VOLTAGE CONTROL

The Switching Arrangements. The control switch, mounted either at the back of the headlamp or on the instrument panel, has the following positions where automatic voltage control is not fitted—

"Off"   Lamps off and dynamo not charging.
"C"   Lamps off and dynamo giving about one-half its normal output.
"H"   Headlamp (main bulb), tail lamp and sidecar lamp, when fitted, on; dynamo giving maximum output.
"L"   The pilot bulb is on and the other lamps are off; dynamo giving maximum output.

Where automatic voltage control is provided there are only three switch positions, namely, "Off," "L," and "H." In all three positions the dynamo gives a controlled output as already explained. During daylight running with the battery well charged the dynamo gives only a trickle charge and the ammeter may show only 1 or 2 amperes.

The Ammeter. This instrument shows the amount of current flowing into or from the battery; it gives an indication that the equipment is working in a satisfactory manner.

1946-9 Models. As previously mentioned the electrical equipment on the 1946-9 Triumph models consists of a separate dynamo and magneto equipment. The several components comprise the dynamo, battery, magneto, ammeter and lamps, the ammeter, switch and lighting switch being mounted on the instrument panel situated on top of the petrol tank.

The dynamo is of the compensated voltage control type. It works in conjunction with a regulator unit which is mounted together with the cut-out. No adjustment is required, as the regulator and cut-out units are correctly set in the Lucas factory. It is the regulator which provides a completely automatic control; the output of the dynamo varies according to the load on the battery and its state of charge. Normally during daylight running the dynamo gives only a trickle charge with the result that the ammeter reading is usually no more than 1 or 2 amperes. Immediately after switching on the headlamp it is possible that a discharge reading is noticed. As a rule this only happens after a long run when the battery voltage is high; the battery voltage drops after a short time and the regulator comes into action, causing the dynamo output to balance the lamp load.

The battery is a Lucas 6-volt lead-acid type. A D142 type Lucas headlamp is fitted as standard.

Maintenance of Equipment

The electrical equipment of the motor-cycle requires regular inspection, together with occasional cleaning and adjustment of some of the parts.

The Battery. Once a month the vent plugs should be removed and the height of the acid solution noted. If below the top of the plates, distilled water should be added to bring the liquid to the top of the separators. If any solution has been spilled it should be made good by the addition of dilute sulphuric acid solution of the same specific density as that in the cell to which it is added. When examining the battery a naked light should not be used—an explosion is liable to occur, because oxygen and hydrogen are both given off.

In the event of the battery being stored for some time arrangements should be made for it to be given a small charge from a separate source of electrical energy about every two weeks; otherwise the battery may be permanently ruined.

The specific gravity of the acid solution should be tested about once a month, a hydrometer being used for the purpose. The specific gravity figures are as follows: When fully charged, 1·250 to 1·300; when half discharged, 1·150–1·250; and when fully discharged, below 1·150. These density figures refer to a temperature of 60° F. A reading should be taken from each cell; if one cell reading differs greatly from the others it suggests that some of the acid has been spilled or has leaked out, or there may be a short

LIGHTING AND ELECTRICAL FITTINGS

between the plates. In the latter case the battery should be examined by a Service Depot.

The Charging Switch. The amount of charging the battery will require depends upon the extent to which the lamps are used. As a rough guide it is suggested that the switch should be left in the "C" position for about one hour daily, and this time should only be increased when there is a considerable amount of night riding, or when the battery is known to be more than half discharged. The foregoing applies, of course, only to those models without automatic voltage control. Where a regulator unit is provided, you can forget all about charging. Make proper use of the ignition switch (see page 7) on coil ignition models and remember that the red warning lamp is not put there as an ornament. Never leave the machine stationary with the red lamp aglow. Should the bulb of the warning lamp fail, this does not affect the functioning of the coil ignition system, but a new 2·5 volt, 0·02 amp. bulb should be fitted as soon as possible.

The Voltage Control Unit. This is sealed by the makers and should not be tampered with, the only likely trouble being oxidizing or welding together of the contacts due to accidental crossing of the dynamo positive and field leads. Keep the battery connexions clean and tight and see that the dynamo to regulator connexions are sound. The voltage control regulator should be changed if a Lucas "Nife" battery is fitted in place of the standard lead-acid type.

The Coil. No attention is needed except to clean occasionally the exterior, particularly the space between the terminals, and to keep the connexions done up tight.

The Dynamo. Always disconnect the positive lead of the battery before removing the dynamo cover. This lead, from the positive battery terminal, is connected to the lead from the switch by means of a brass connector. The connector is insulated by a rubber shield, and this must be pushed back to expose the cable connector.

The Brushes. The dynamo brushes should be examined occasionally; their removal from the holders is easy when the spring lever is held to the side. The brushes should slide freely in their holders and also make good contact with the commutator. Dirty or greasy brushes can be cleaned with a petrol-moistened cloth. It should be noted that the brushes must be replaced in their original positions. When worn, new brushes—of the same make—

should be fitted. These should be properly bedded at a Lucas Service Depot.

The Commutator. This part of the dynamo should be kept clean and free from oil. To clean, remove one of the main brushes from its holder, insert a fine duster, hold this in position against the commutator with a piece of wood, and rotate the engine so as to turn the armature. The normal colour of a "healthy" commutator is dark bronze. If the segments are very dirty, use a duster

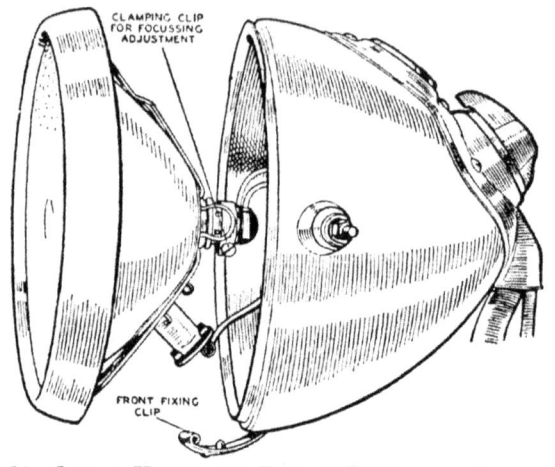

FIG. 31. LUCAS HEADLAMP TYPE DU142 WITH FRONT AND REFLECTOR DETACHED

moistened in petrol, or if necessary, fine glass-paper. If glass-paper is used, blow out the particles with a tyre pump.

Focusing Headlamp (DU142, D142 Type). The Lucas DU142, D142 type headlamps are fitted on 1935-9 models, but earlier machines employ the H52 type shown in Fig. 32. The DU142 and D142 type lamps are similar except that the former is used on models without an instrument panel, while the latter is fitted on machines with an instrument panel. The ammeter and lighting switch are incorporated on the back of the H52 and the DU142 headlamp.

To focus the main bulb (DU142, D142), first remove the lamp front and reflector by pressing back the fixing clip. Next slacken the clamping screw which secures the bulb-holder and move the holder and bulb until the correct focus is obtained. The clamping screw should afterwards be retightened. The bulb-holder may be detached by pressing back the two securing springs. Always locate the top of the rim first when replacing the lamp front and reflector.

LIGHTING AND ELECTRICAL FITTINGS

The Lucas headlamp, type H52, is shown in a dismantled state in Fig. 32. To remove the lamp front, press the front rim evenly and then rotate to the left. When removing the main bulb for replacement, screw it out two or three turns in an anti-clockwise direction; then the bulb can be withdrawn easily. When fitting the new bulb, see it is the right way round—with the dipped beam filament above the centre filament.

To focus the headlamp turn the bulb in a clockwise direction to move it inwards, and vice versa. The best position can easily be

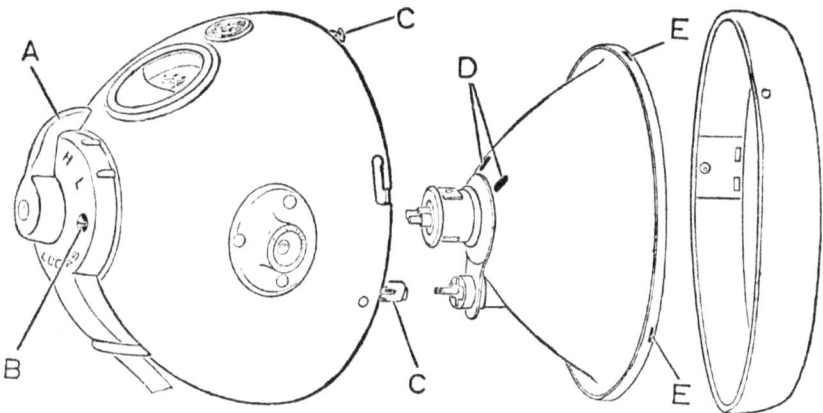

FIG. 32. LUCAS HEADLAMP TYPE H52 DISMANTLED

A—Switch.
B—Fixing screw.
C—Reflector supports.
D—Apertures through which light passes to illuminate ammeter.
E—Slots in reflector rim.

found by trial. In adjusting the bulb it should be given a complete turn, so that the filaments are in the correct position; the spring stop in the bulb-holder indicates each complete turn by a click action.

The following Lucas replacement bulbs are recommended—

	No.	Watts	
Headlamp (driving and dipped beam lights)	70	24 & 24	Special double filament gas-filled
Headlamp (pilot light), sidecar, tail and stop lamps	200	3	Centre contact bulb
Panel lamps	200	3	Centre contact bulb

Wiring of the Equipment. Before making any alteration to the wiring, or removing the switch from the back of the headlamp or from the instrument panel, disconnect the positive lead at the battery. All leads to the DU142 type headlamp are taken direct to the switch, which together with the ammeter is incorporated in a small panel. To remove this panel it is only necessary to remove the three securing screws.

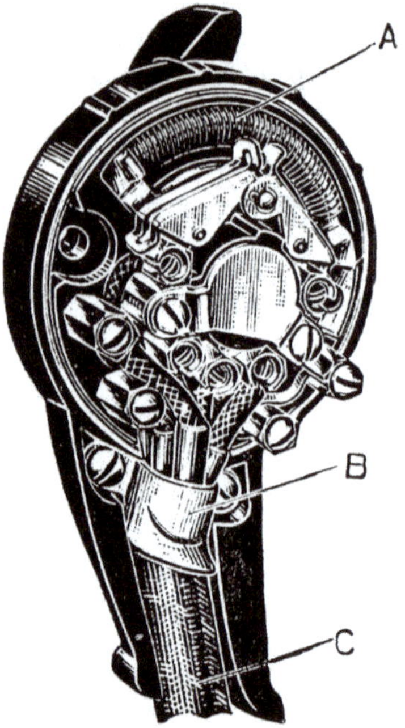

It is possible to identify the ends of all cables in the lighting system by means of coloured sleevings. Wiring diagrams are given on pages 59-62 and these explain the connexions and also the colour scheme. To make a connexion to the switch, proceed as follows. First bare about $\frac{3}{8}$ in. of the cable, twist the strands together and turn back about $\frac{1}{8}$ in. so as to form a small ball. Then remove the grub screw from the terminal concerned and insert the wire so that the ball fits in the terminal post. The grub screw should now be refitted and tightened so as to compress the ball and make a good electrical connexion.

To make a connexion to the dynamo or regulator terminals on 1937-9 models, first slacken the fixing screw on the terminal block and remove the clamping plate. Next withdraw the metal sleeves in each terminal. Pass about one inch of cable through the clamping plate holes and bare the ends for a distance of about $\frac{3}{8}$ in. Now place the metal sleeves over the cables, bend back the wire over the sleeves, and push them right home into their appropriate terminals. Afterwards screw down the clamping plate. It is essential that the leads connected to the "D" and "F" terminals of the dynamo or regulator should not be reversed, and to prevent this being done inadvertently, the screw in the dynamo terminal block is off-centre and the screws which secure the terminal clamping plate of the regulator are of different size.

FIG. 33. SWITCH REMOVED FROM BACK OF HEADLAMP TYPE H52
A—Resistance.
B—Clamping clip for cables.
C—Cable harness.

Care of the Magneto Portion of the Lucas "Magdyno." The contact breaker should be examined occasionally. The contacts

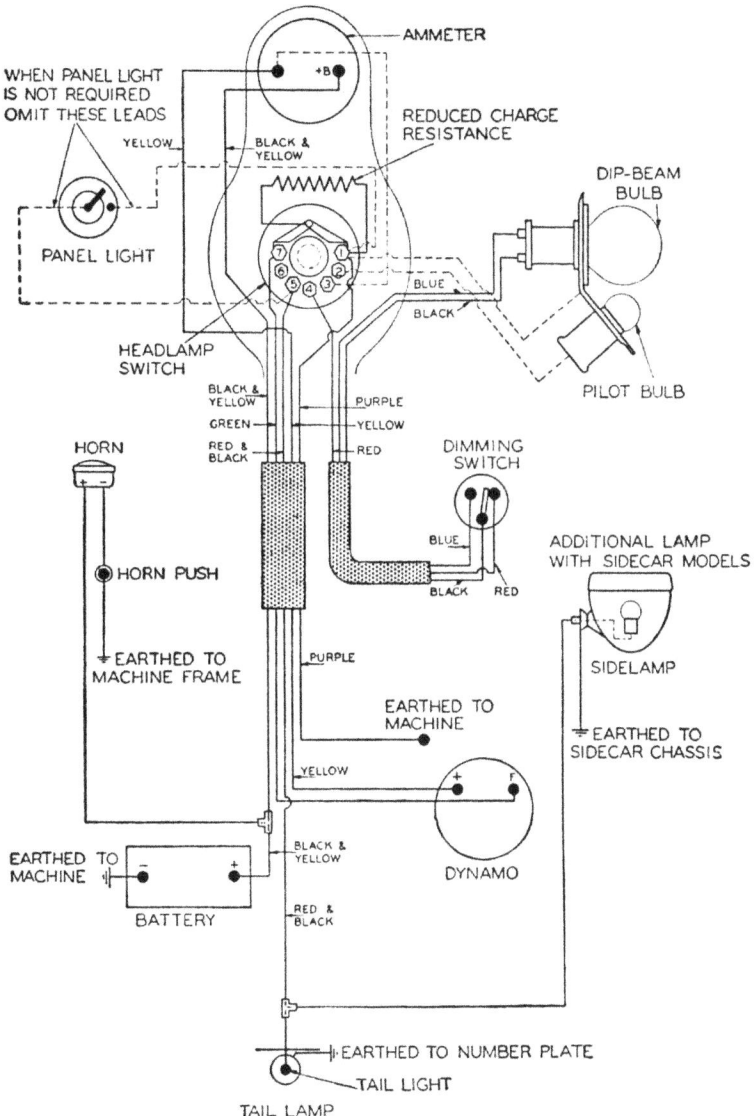

Fig. 34. Wiring Diagram for 1935-6 Lucas "Magdyno" Lighting Equipment without Automatic Voltage Control and Instrument Panel
(*Messrs. Joseph Lucas, Ltd.*)

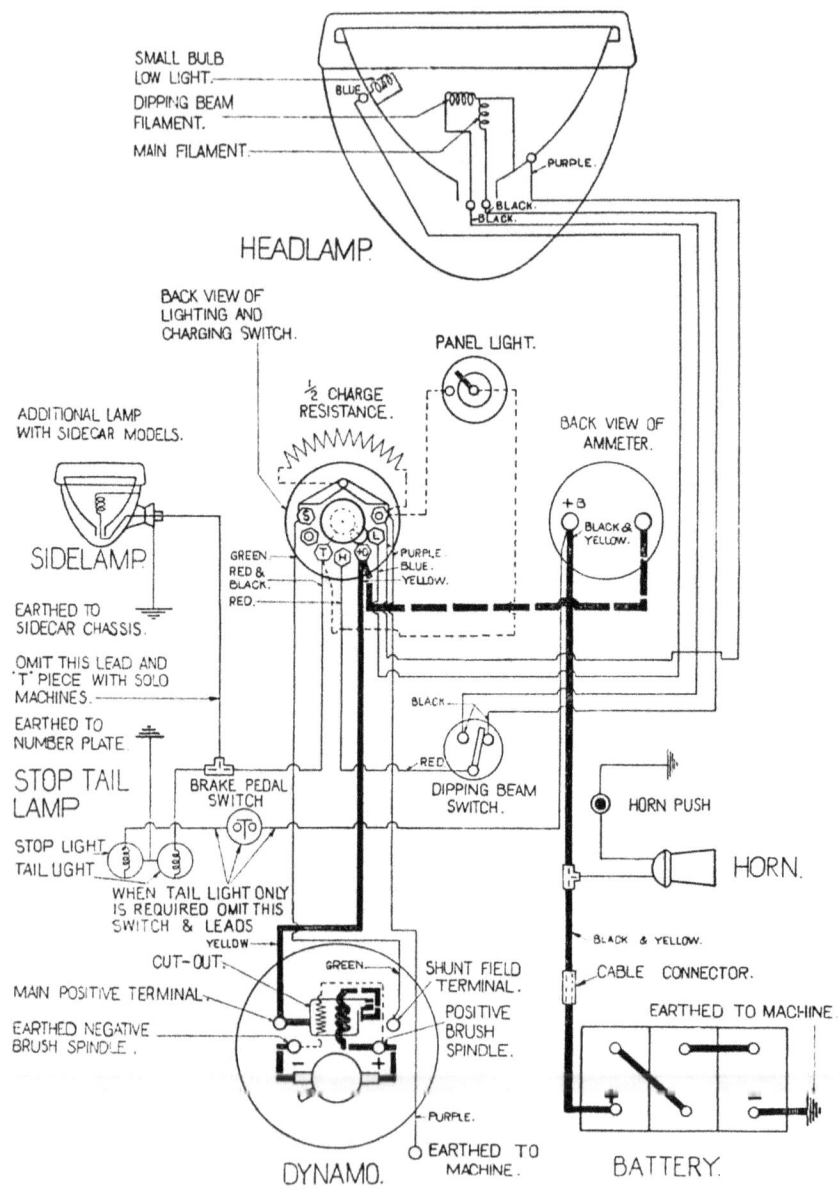

Fig. 35. Wiring Diagram for 1935-6 Lucas "Magdyno" Lighting Equipment (with Instrument Panel) without Automatic Voltage Control

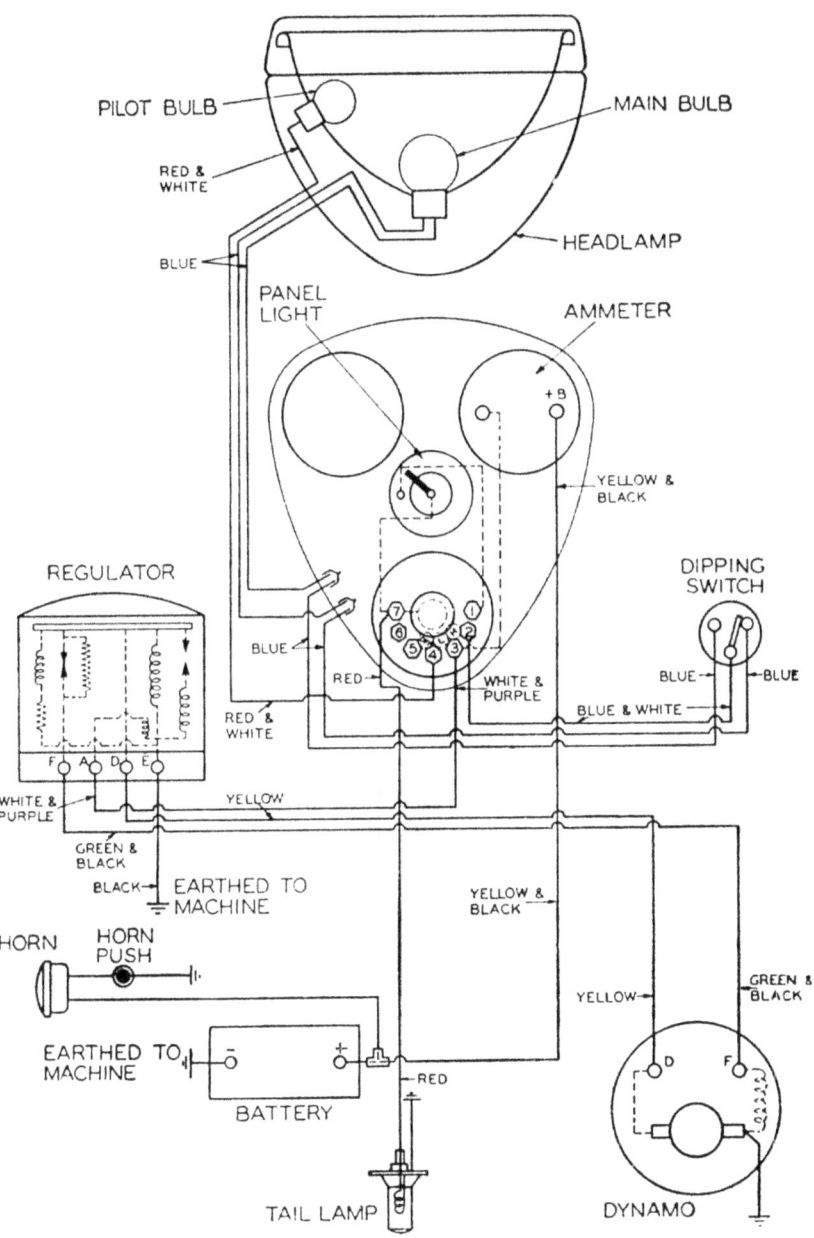

Fig. 36. Wiring Diagram for 1937-9 Lucas "Magdyno" Lighting Equipment with Automatic Voltage Control and Instrument Panel

(*Messrs. Joseph Lucas, Ltd.*)

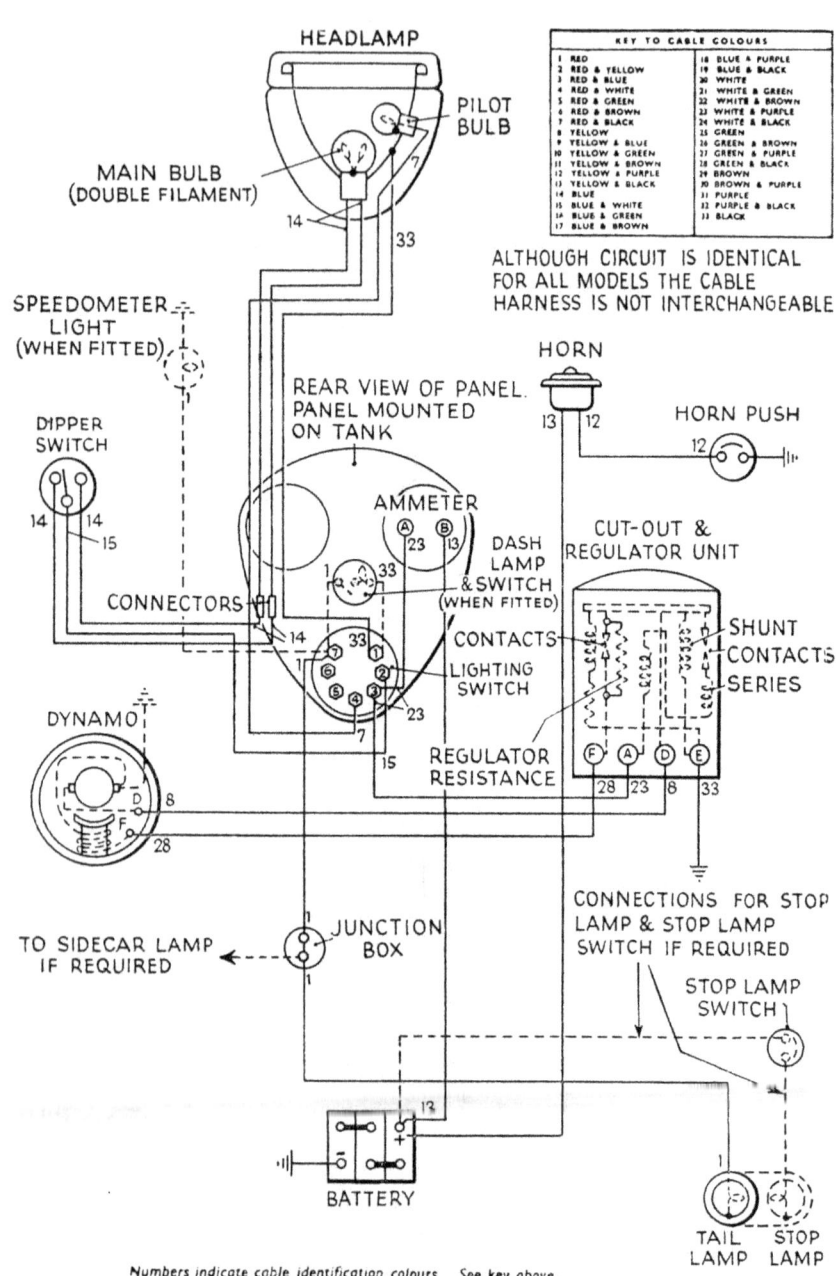

FIG. 37. WIRING DIAGRAM FOR 1946 MODELS LUCAS SEPARATE DYNAMO AND MAGNETO EQUIPMENT

LIGHTING AND ELECTRICAL FITTINGS 63

(Figs. 8, 29) must be kept clean and free from any traces of oil. If burned or blackened they may be cleaned. The procedure in the case of a (1935–6) ring cam type contact breaker is as follows.

Withdraw contact breaker from its housing by unscrewing the hexagon-headed screw G by means of the magneto spanner, when the whole can be pulled off the tapered shaft. By pushing aside spring H the rocker arm can be prised off its bearings, then it is

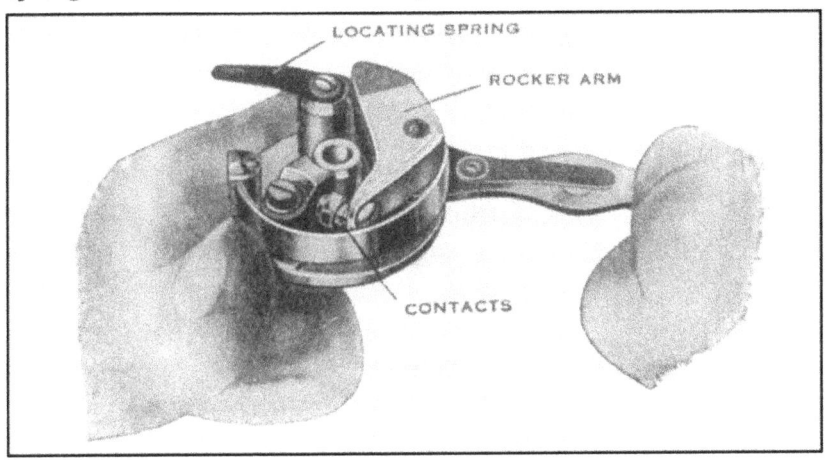

FIG. 38. 1935–6 CONTACT BREAKER SHOWING METHOD OF REMOVING ROCKER ARM FOR CLEANING CONTACTS

possible to begin cleaning the contacts (see also Fig. 38). Polish with very fine carborundum stone or fine emery cloth, and afterwards wipe with a petrol-moistened cloth. Before replacing the contact breaker, see that the rocker arm works quite freely; if there is any sluggishness, clean the bearing pin with fine emery-cloth and add a spot of oil. Lubrication of the ring cam is dealt with on page 69. It is also important that care should be taken to ensure that the projecting key on the tapered portion of the contact-breaker base engages with the key-way cut in the armature spindle.

With a face cam type contact breaker (Fig. 9) fitted on 1937–9 singles the above instructions for cleaning the contacts apply, but in this case to render the contacts accessible for cleaning it is necessary to remove the spring arm carrying the moving contact. When replacing this arm it is most important to make sure that the small backing spring is refitted correctly, that is, under the securing screw and washer with the bent portion facing *outwards*.

Remove the pick-up R, Fig. 29, wipe the moulding clean with a dry cloth, and see that the carbon brush moves freely in its holder, being careful not to stretch the brush spring unduly. With the pick-up removed, carefully clean the slip ring and flanges by holding a soft cloth on the ring by means of a suitably-shaped piece of wood, while the engine is turned slowly over.

The contacts of the contact breaker only require adjustment at long intervals, unless the gap varies considerably from the gauge. When adjustment is necessary, turn the engine slowly until the points are seen to be fully opened, then slacken the locking

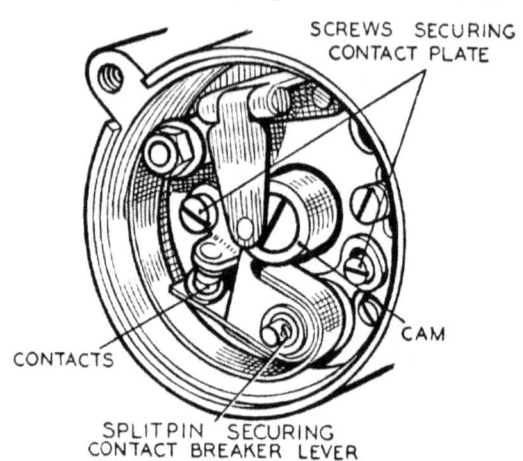

FIG. 39. CONTACT BREAKER ON LUCAS DYNAMO
(Provided on 1939 coil ignition models)

nut (Figs. 9, 29), and rotate the contact screw by its hexagon head until the gap is set to the gauge on the magneto spanner (0·012 in.); then tighten the locking nut.

The Dynamo Contact Breaker (Coil Ignition). Once in a while the moulded cover should be taken off and the contacts of the contact breaker (Fig. 39) examined. As in the case of the Lucas "Magdyno," the contact breaker on the coil ignition models (2HC, 3SC) must always be kept scrupulously clean and free from oil. Blackened or burned contacts should be cleaned with fine carborundum stone or, if unavailable, fine emery-cloth. Wipe the contacts with a clean cloth moistened with petrol afterwards. To clean very dirty or pitted contacts, it is best to remove the rocker arm from its housing by removing the collar and nut securing the spring and the split pin securing the arm and lifting the rocker arm off its pin. Having cleaned the contacts, replace the rocker arm, refit the collar and nut, also the split pin securing the contact breaker arm, and finally check and, if necessary, adjust the gap between the contacts.

As a rule it is seldom necessary to alter the contact breaker gap

LIGHTING AND ELECTRICAL FITTINGS 65

which is carefully adjusted by the makers. However, as that part of the rocker arm which contacts with the cam gradually wears, the size of the gap decreases and must be rectified. The correct gap is 0·008 in. to 0·010 in., and every few hundred miles it is a good plan to turn the engine over slowly by hand until the contacts are wide open and insert a feeler gauge of the correct thickness between them. The blade of the gauge should slide between the points without binding. However, unless the gap varies appreciably from the gauge, it is not advisable to alter the setting. If an adjustment is needed, this may be effected in the following manner: when the contacts are wide open, slacken the screws securing the plate which carries the stationary contact and then carefully adjust the position of the plate until the correct " break " at the contacts is obtained. Afterwards tighten the securing screws and again check the "break." Finally replace the moulded cover. When doing this it is most important to verify that the hinged spring blade on the contact breaker makes good contact with the condenser case inside the cover. Arcing and burning away of the contacts will occur unless the blade presses firmly against the case. Lubrication is referred to on page 68.

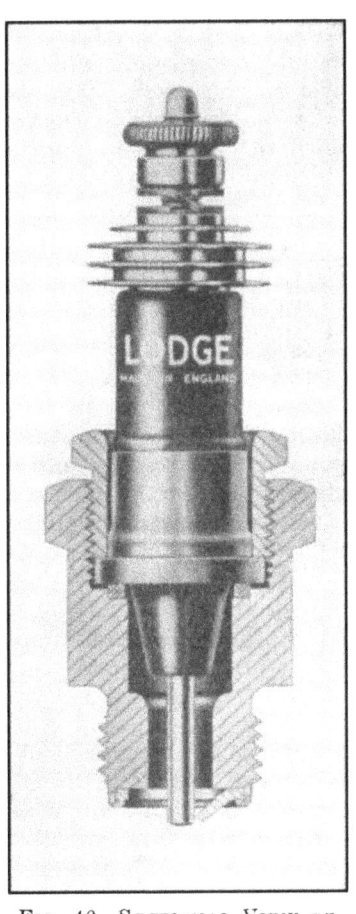

FIG. 40. SECTIONAL VIEW OF LODGE PLUG (TYPE H1)

The Sparking Plug. In order to obtain maximum performance and reliability it is important always to run on a good quality sparking plug such as the Lodge or K.L.G. The use of an inferior plug is apt to cause a large amount of bother and reduce engine performance. Most 1937–9 Triumph models require plugs of the 14 mm. size, but many earlier type engines require 18 mm. plugs. The recommendations of the Triumph Engineering Co., Ltd., are given in the table which appears on the following page.

The electrode points slowly burn away under the heat of

combustion, and it is therefore advisable as a matter of routine occasionally to remove the plug from the cylinder head and check the gap between the electrode points with a suitable feeler gauge. The correct gap on all "Magdyno" ignition models is 0·018 in. to 0·020 in. In the case of coil ignition models the correct gap is 0·022 in., but if K.L.G. plugs are fitted the gap should not exceed 0·020 in., irrespective of the type of ignition system employed. The blade of the feeler gauge should just slide between the centre electrode and the outer (earth) electrode(s) without causing the points to spring. An excellent combined key ring and plug gap setting gauge is obtainable *free* from Messrs.

	Lodge	K.L.G.	Champion
All models fitted with 18 mm. plugs	H1	M.50	16
All other S.V.	C3	F.70	L.10
All O.H.V. singles	H.14	F.80	L.10S
Speed Twin	H.14	F.80	L.10S
T100	H.14	F.100	L.11S

Lodge Plugs Ltd., of Rugby, on receipt of a 2½d. stamp to cover postage. Where the gap at the points is found to be excessive, the outer (earth) electrode point(s) should be gently pressed inwards towards the centre electrode. This may readily be done with the aid of a pair of sharp-nosed pliers.

The plug is prone to becoming oiled up (especially in the case of new engines), sooty or carbonized, and must therefore be from time to time dismantled and cleaned. Where a plug is only slightly dirty, a marked improvement can usually be obtained by merely brightening up the electrode point(s) with a pen-knife or some fine emery-cloth. But if the plug is dirty inside it is best to dismantle it for thorough cleaning. Some K.L.G. plugs are of the two-piece type and in this case no attempt must be made to detach the gland nut from the insulated centre. To dismantle a three-piece plug, use a special plug detacher or else a vice and box spanner. If a vice is used, do not on any account allow the vice jaws to exert pressure on the hexagon of the metal body. Tighten the vice just sufficiently to prevent the plug turning. As soon as the gland nut has been unscrewed with a box spanner, the centre insulated electrode may be withdrawn. Wipe the whole of the mica insulation with a clean rag moistened with petrol until the insulation is perfectly clean, but do not scrape it clean. Carbon or soot deposits may be removed by scraping from the metal parts. Afterwards rinse the body of the plug in petrol and dry. Clean the plug points most carefully with a knife or wire brush. When reassembling the plug, make absolutely certain that the internal washer (see Fig. 40) is seating properly, that

LIGHTING AND ELECTRICAL FITTINGS

there is no grit in the joint, and that the gland nut is firmly retightened. Finally check the gap at the points and refit the plug in the engine.

MAINTENANCE OF 1946–9 EQUIPMENT

Much of what has been said regarding maintenance of the electrical equipment of the pre-war models applies equally to the 1946 and 1949 Triumphs, but as the equipment consists of a separate dynamo and magneto a few further details may be given.

The Battery. The level of the acid in the cells should be examined about once a month. To do this, remove the battery lid and unscrew the filler caps. Distilled water should be added, if necessary, to bring the acid level with the tops of the separators. An inflammable gas may be given off by the cells, so a naked light should not be held near the vent holes. At the same time, it is advisable to determine the condition of the battery by taking readings with a hydrometer. The specific gravity readings indicate: 1·250–1·300, battery fully charged; 1·150–1·250, about half discharged; below 1·150 fully discharged. These figures are applicable when the temperature of the solution is about 60° F. The readings for each of the three cells should be approximately the same; if one is very different from the other two, it is probable that acid has spilled or leaked from this particular cell, or there may be a short circuit between the plates. In the event of this happening, the battery should be examined by a service depot.

The battery should not be left in a discharged condition for any appreciable length of time. If the motor-cycle is out of commission for any time, charge the battery fully, and about every two weeks give it a short freshening charge to prevent any risk of permanent sulphation of the plates.

The Dynamo. Remove the cover of the dynamo about every six months so that the commutator and brushes may be inspected. The brushes must make firm contact with the commutator; they are held in boxes by means of springs; the brush should be moved to see that it is free to slide in its holder; if not, remove it and clean with a cloth moistened with petrol. The brushes must be replaced in their original position, or they will not bed properly. The commutator should be free from oil or dirt; its surface should be highly polished. If dirty or blackened, clean by pressing a fine duster against it while the engine is slowly turned over by hand. Moisten the duster with petrol if the commutator is very dirty.

The Magneto. The contact breaker of the magneto should be inspected at intervals. It is of paramount importance that the contacts be kept clean and free from oil or grease. Clean with fine carborundum stone if burned or blackened; use fine emery cloth if not available. Wipe with a cloth moistened with petrol after cleaning. If the points are in a very bad state, the contact breaker assembly should be removed from its housing and the rocker arm removed so that both contacts may be cleaned properly. After cleaning refit the rocker arm and replace the contact breaker in its housing. The gap should be checked and, if necessary, adjusted to 0·012 in.; a spanner and feeler gauge are provided for this purpose in the tool kit.

If the magneto is to be removed it is necessary to take off the timing case cover. There is a peg on the fibre gear which serves as a stop for the fully advanced position. To remove the driving gear and auto advance mechanism, place a 5/16 in. B.S.F. nut between one of the fixed bobweight lips and a movable lip. This will prevent the rotatable mechanism coming into contact with the fully advanced peg. Next the shaft nut should be unscrewed with a slow, but firm, turning movement (R.H. thread) to release it from the shaft and, at the same time, withdraw the assembly. Although no key is fitted the shaft has a key-way cut in it. Then remove the two H.T. leads from the plug ends and disconnect the cut-out lead. When the three clamping nuts have been removed, the magneto can be taken off.

When replacing the magneto, jointing compound should be smeared on the magneto face; then position over the three studs; replace the three nuts, and tighten. Fit the auto-advance and retard mechanism gear; time the magneto to engine and tighten central nut. Replace contact breaker cover, earth lead and H.T. cables to plugs. Clean the timing cover and crankcase faces and smear jointing compound lightly over the timing cover face before replacing.

The Sparking Plugs. The plugs fitted to the 350 c.c. 1946 models are Champion L.10.MOD, and Lodge H.14.S to the 500 c.c. machines. The recommended plug gap is 15–18 thous. It is necessary to clean the plugs periodically, by washing them in petrol and removing any deposit from the electrodes, but unless absolutely essential they should not be dismantled. The plugs provided on all models are suitable for average give-and-take running; for continued high speed work, however, it may be advisable to fit a harder plug to the faster engines.

Dynamo Lubrication (Coil Ignition Models). It is advisable about every 1000 miles to smear the surface of the steel cam with some Mobilgrease No. 2. Be careful not to over lubricate. Every 5000 miles remove the rocker arm from the contact breaker (see page 63) and lightly smear the pivot with a little Mobilgrease No. 2.

LIGHTING AND ELECTRICAL FITTINGS

The dynamo bearings are packed with grease during assembly and this should suffice until the motor-cycle is stripped for a general overhaul, at which time it is advisable to return the complete dynamo to the nearest Lucas Service Depot for cleaning, adjustment, and further greasing of the bearings. Where a lubricator is provided on the commutator cover (Fig. 9), insert a few drops of thin machine oil every 2000 miles.

"Magdyno" Lubrication. The foregoing remarks concerning the lubrication of the dynamo bearings apply also to the dynamo portion of the Lucas "Magdyno." In the case of a ring cam type contact breaker (1935-6) the cam is lubricated by a felt wick contained in a hole in the cam, and every 5000 miles the cam ring should be withdrawn and a few drops of thin machine oil added to the wick. At the same time, push aside the locating spring (Fig. 29), prise the rocker arm off its pivot, and lightly smear the pivot bearing with a little Mobilgrease No. 2. On earlier ring cam type contact breakers no felt wick is provided in the cam, and it is necessary to smear a little oil on the surface from time to time. It is most important, however, in the case of all contact breakers never to allow any oil or grease to get on the contacts or near them.

With a face cam type of contact breaker (1937–9) lubrication of the cam is effected by means of a wick housed in the contact breaker base. About every 5000 miles add a few drops of thin machine oil to the wick. The screw which carries the wick may be withdrawn after removing the spring arm carrying the moving contact (Fig. 9). Also remove the tappet which operates the contact breaker spring and lightly smear it with thin machine oil. It is important when replacing the spring arm to make sure that the small backing spring is correctly refitted.

Lubricating 1946 and 1949 Models. A few drops of good grade thin machine oil should be given to the lubricator at the commutator end bracket every 4000–5000 miles. The bearing at the driving end is packed with grease and this need not be renewed until the machine is taken down for a general overhaul. The magneto also requires lubricating about every 5000 miles. If the cam is of the ring type it is lubricated by a length of felt contained in the contact breaker housing. A small hole in the cam, fitted with a wick, allows oil to find its way on to the surface of the cam. Every 5000 miles, withdraw the cam ring and add a few drops of thin machine oil to the cam. At the same time, push aside the locating spring, prise the rocker arm off its bearing and smear the bearing lightly with petroleum jelly. If the cam is of the face type, the cam is lubricated by a wick contained in the contact breaker base. Add a few drops of thin machine oil to the wick every 5000 miles. To gain access to the wick, remove the spring arm carrying the moving contact and withdraw the screw carrying the wick. At the same time, remove the tappet which operates the contact breaker spring and smear it lightly with thin machine oil. When replacing, be careful to see that the small backing spring is fitted immediately under the securing screw and spring washer, and with bent portion facing outwards. The bearings are packed with grease and do not require attention until the machine is dismantled for cleaning, adjustment and repacking the bearings with grease.

CHAPTER VI

BICYCLE PARTS: ADJUSTMENTS AND DISMANTLING

ADJUSTING and dismantling the bicycle parts occasion some motor-cyclists more concern than attending to the engine and transmission. There are others who tend to neglect these units. Since the whole question is of some importance it is dealt with in a separate chapter.

Front Forks (1935-6). End play can be taken up by adjusting the link axles. The pinch bolts (Fig. 28) on the lower links should first

FIG. 41. ARRANGEMENT OF STEERING HEAD (1935-6)

be slackened and then the nuts on the spindles. The latter should then be rotated clockwise until all end play has been taken up, then it should be eased back slightly, when the nuts and bolts should be secured. Access to the front top spindle is only possible when the fork dampers are dismantled, but this is an obvious operation (Fig. 41).

It should be noted that there are neither dampers nor link pinch bolts in the case of Model L2/1.

Front Forks (1937-9). End play should be taken up in the fork spindles as soon as it is detected because play affects the steering and also the action of the shock-absorbers. On new machines the spindle bearings and shock-absorbers settle down after about 1000 miles, and therefore at the end of this period and subsequently about every 2000 miles the front forks should be examined for spindle play. The correct adjustment of the spindles is such that the knurled edge washers are just free to spin. There should be no general looseness. To adjust each spindle, loosen the end nuts and then turn with a spanner the

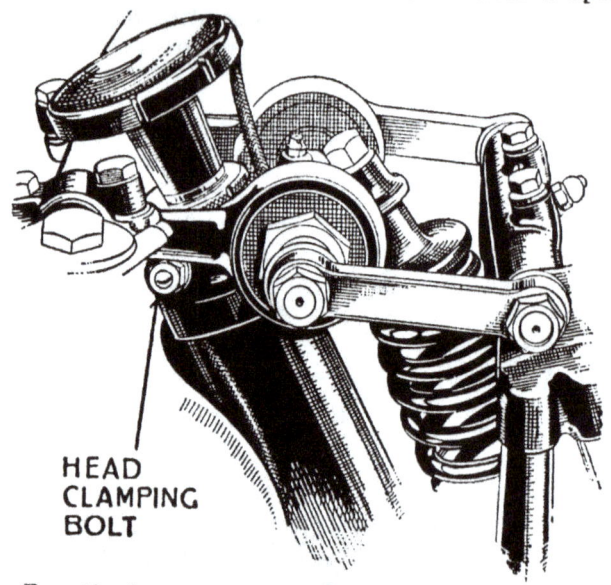

FIG. 42. ARRANGEMENT OF STEERING HEAD (1937-9)
An illustration showing the steering head and front forks on the 1935-6 models is to be found on page 71

squared end until the above-mentioned adjustment is obtained. Retighten the locknuts and again check the adjustment.

Front Forks (1946 and 1949). The Triumph hydraulically controlled telescopic fork requires no regular maintenance, and no lubrication is necessary; an occasional check of the external nuts is all that is needed. Rather more frequently, however, the drain plug and pressure valve retaining screw should be checked. These are both located in the lower end of the bottom member. If any great quantity of oil is lost when changing the fibre and copper washers, the forks should be completely drained and refilled; refill each fork leg with 100 c.c. of oil. This can be done by unscrewing the large cap nuts, but care should be taken that they are not detached from the rod. This operation is discussed in the paragraph regarding changing the fork spring.

BICYCLE PARTS

The improved Triumph telescopic fork, as incorporated in the 3T de Luxe, Speed Twin, and Tiger "100" standard models, and in the "Trophy" and "Grand Prix" 1949 models, with six inches of hydraulically damped movement, sets a high standard of controllability and comfort. The sectioned drawing, Fig. 43, shows the internal arrangement. The long supple fork springs are enclosed inside the stanchions, and this enables these latter vital components to be of maximum possible diameter and strength. No adjustments of any kind have to be made by the rider, and maintenance is reduced to checking the oil level every 10,000 miles. To assist in maintenance a screw-plug is fitted to each stanchion inside the nacelle, enabling oil to be introduced into the forks through the headlamp aperture.

Sidecar Fork Spring. The fork springs must be changed if the machine is used with a sidecar. The following is the correct procedure: 1. Disconnect front brake cable. 2. Raise the front wheel clear of the ground, 3–4 in. — a box of suitable height can be placed under the crankcase. 3. Unscrew both large nuts fitted to the top of the fork tube. Then remove the box. With the forks under compression the large nuts will

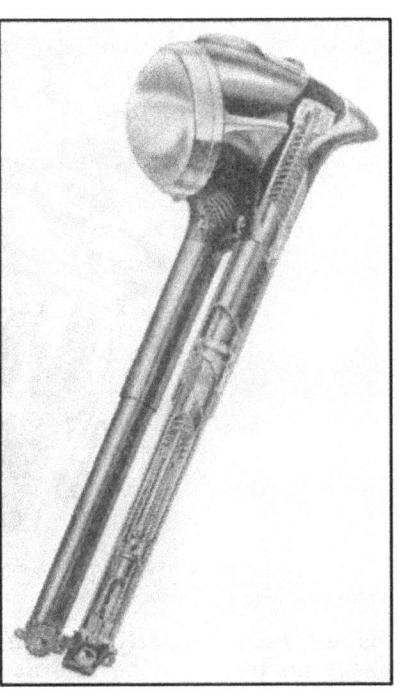

Fig. 43 Triumph Telescopic Fork

be seen to be attached to a rod over which the springs are fitted. 4. Depress the spring so that the rod can be gripped with a pair of pliers. The large nut can then be screwed off the rod and the spring extracted. The other fork leg is dealt with in the same manner. After fitting the sidecar strength springs, assemble the fork by the reverse procedure; make certain that both nuts are tight on the rods and in the head lug.

Steering. When adjusting the steering head bearing it is necessary to support the machine on the rear stand and also on a box placed underneath the crankcase, so as to relieve the races of all external influence, and also to slacken off the steering damper.

To adjust, ease the head clip pinch bolt—this is at the rear of the clip and immediately beneath the handlebar centre, as shown in Fig. 42—then with the special "C" spanner in the tool kit turn the collar immediately below the steering damper knob clockwise or anti-clockwise, according to whether it is desired to take up or increase play respectively. The correct adjustment of the steering head is such that on grasping the lower ends of the fork

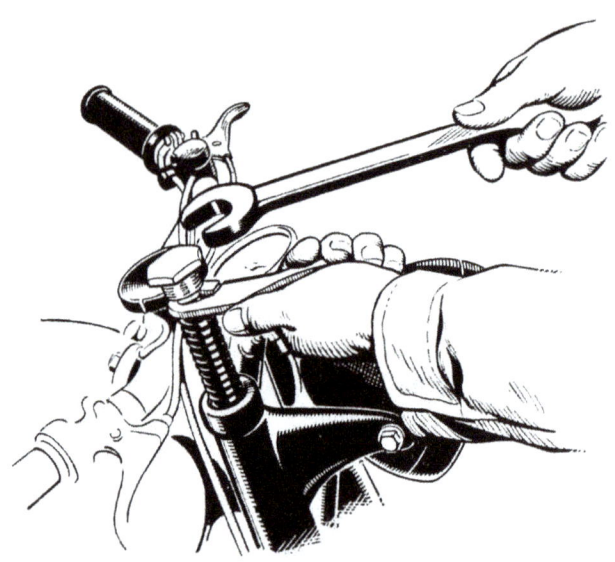

Fig. 44. Method of Removing the Fork Main Springs

blades and alternately pushing and pulling the forks towards the head, no play can be felt at the head upper bearing, yet the forks can be turned freely by means of the handlebars without any suspicion of binding. After obtaining the correct adjustment, securely retighten the head clamping bolt (Fig. 42). Before making an adjustment it is a good plan to tighten the fork shock-absorbers or dampers, so that when the weight of the machine is taken off the front forks by placing a box beneath the frame cradle, the fork spring does not expand and bear against the frame.

Steering (1946-9). Steering and road holding are both adversely affected if the steering head bearings are not maintained in correct adjustment. If the adjustment is too tight, excessive friction results; if too slack, the ball races become pitted and their early replacement is necessary.

BICYCLE PARTS 75

Triumphs recommend the following procedure when adjusting the steering head: 1. Slacken steering damper right off. 2. Support front forks clear of the ground by placing a box under the frame cradle. 3. Grasp the lower end of the front forks and, by alternately pushing and pulling, feel for traces of play in the head. 4. Check freedom of steering by turning from left to right and back again. There should be no play registered by the

FIG. 45. TESTING THE ADJUSTMENT OF THE STEERING HEAD RACES

first test, but the second test must register absolute freedom of movement. Any adjustment is carried out by slacking off the nut on the head clamping bolt and using the spanner supplied in the tool kit on the sleeve nut which is immediately below the steering damper knob.

Hub Bearings. It is unlikely that the hub bearings will often require adjustment, but if the lateral movement is more than, say $\frac{1}{64}$ in., it should be done. The wheel should be raised off the ground and the brake eased off, and the outer or axle nuts on the spindle should be slackened. In the case of a rear wheel removal of the chain allows for a more accurate adjustment. Loosen the outer of the two nuts inside the fork on the near-side for the front wheel and the off-side for the rear wheel, and rotate the inner nut clockwise until the rim gives a lateral movement or not more than $\frac{1}{64}$ in.; finally secure all the nuts.

The Front Wheel. The removal of the front wheel is a straightforward operation. If it is necessary to dismantle the bearings proceed as follows: remove the adjusting and locknuts from the near-side end of the axle and push out. The nut at the right-hand

Fig. 46. Testing Front Wheel Bearings

end should not be disturbed, unless it is essential to do so for some special reason. The inner spools and the roller cages can be taken clear of the outer rings. These outer rings, which are a press fit in the hub tube, may be driven out by inserting a rod of soft metal from the reverse side abutting against the inner edge of the race; they can be returned in the same way—by pressing them evenly into the housing.

With the 1946 models the front wheel bearings are of the ball bearing type and require no adjustment. The lateral movement should be hardly perceptible (see Fig. 46).

The Rear Wheel. If the rear wheel is of the quickly detachable type it can be removed easily by detaching the tail guard, the nut from the pull out bolt—withdrawing the latter—and easing the

BICYCLE PARTS

wheel off the splines to release. The brake mechanism is left undisturbed. With all other types, remove the chain, by detaching the split link, the outer axle nuts, the tail guard and the brake rod nuts.

In construction the rear wheel is more or less similar to the front wheel, but certain parts are reversed. The adjustment, for

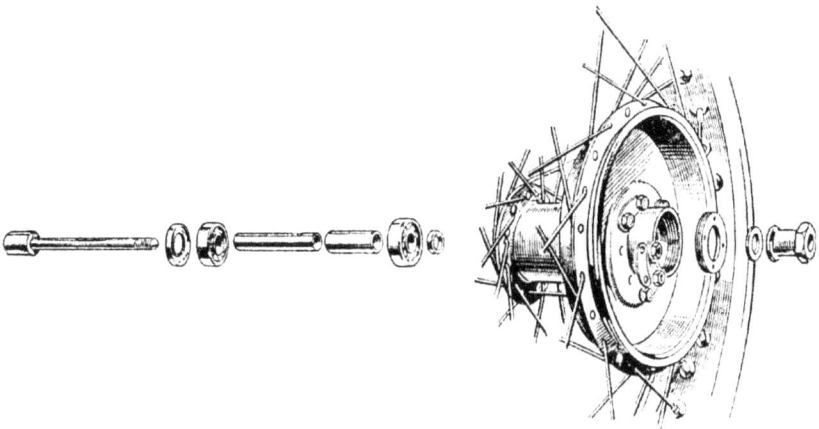

FIG. 47. FRONT WHEEL BEARING ASSEMBLY

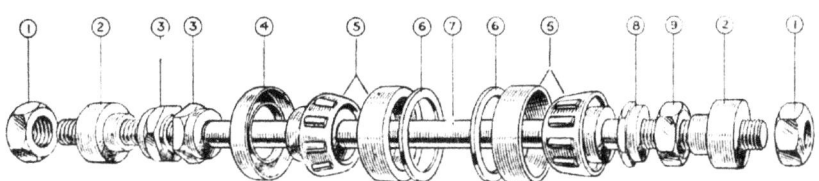

FIG. 48. REAR WHEEL BEARING ASSEMBLY

Showing axle, taper roller bearings and all nuts. The speedometer drive gear-box fits between the nuts numbered 8 and 9 and the rear brake anchor plate between the nuts marked 3

example, is on the off-side, this requiring the axle to be removed to the left, and the anchor plate location is by a spigot to the fork lug.

The rear wheel bearings of the wheels of the 1946 models are of the taper roller type; after tightening the lock nut the lateral movement at the wheel rim should be just perceptible.

When dismantling and assembling the front and rear wheel bearing assemblies of 1946 models, Figs. 47 and 48 should be used as a guide to the correct sequence.

To remove the front wheel, disconnect the brake cable at the lower end; lower the front stand and unscrew spindle nut; slack off wheel spindle pinch bolt on near-side fork and drive spindle out from the off-side. To replace the front wheel, place the wheel between the fork members and enter the wheel spindle from the near-side; gently tap the spindle through until the threaded portion is visible through the opposite form member; fit the bolt to the brake anchor plate, assemble nut to wheel

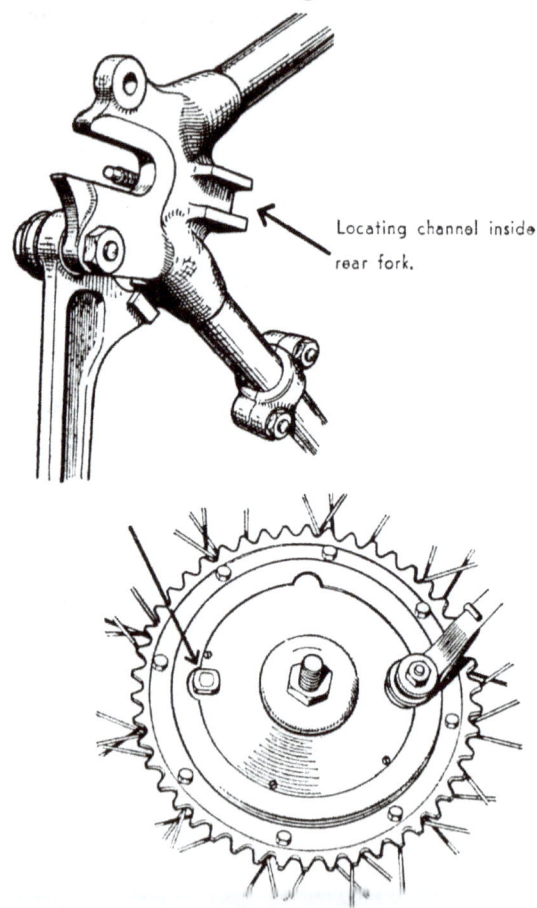

Figs. 49 and 49a. Stud on Rear Brake Anchor Plate which must be located in Rear Fork Channel

spindle and tighten; reposition front stand; grip the handlebars and work the fork movement up and down to align the lower fork members to the fork stanchions; then fit the spindle pinch bolt and the brake attachments.

The removal of the rear wheel is a rather more complicated task. Proceed as follows: Slacken off the nuts securing the tail-guard mudguard stay; remove the two hexagonal-headed screws securing the tailguard to the mudguard blade; remove the tailguard and place at side of the machine. The rear lamp cable need not be removed. Take the spring link out of the chain to break it, and see that the gear-box is not in neutral (if the sprocket is free it may rotate and the chain drops off); screw off the brake adjusting nut; slacken off the two spindle nuts and withdraw the wheel from the fork. The speedometer drive must be disconnected before releasing the wheel. To replace the rear

Fig. 50. Triumph Spring Wheel

wheel, proceed in the reverse order. It is of the greatest importance to see that the stud on the brake anchor plate fits into the locating channel on the inside of the rear fork (see Figs. 49 and 49A).

Reference has previously been made (Chapter IV) to the spring wheel introduced recently. This remarkable springing system has already become popular the world over. It is essentially simple, efficient and reliable. All the moving parts are totally enclosed in a massive aluminium alloy hub, and attached to this is a powerful 8 in. brake. The spring wheel is mounted in the frame in exactly the same way as a normal wheel, and adds only 3 per cent to the total weight of the machine.

The spindle remains stationary bolted into the frame as usual while the hub and wheel move on a curved path taken from the centre of the gear-box sprocket; this ensures that chain tension remains constant at all times The movement is controlled by springs, two below the spindle and one above. Details are shown in Fig. 50.

THE BOOK OF THE TRIUMPH

The Tyres. The tyres must be maintained at the correct inflation pressure if they are to provide safe and comfortable riding, a long life and immunity from trouble. The pressure

Lb. per sq. in. minimum inflation pressure	Tyre Size	Front Tyres	Rear Tyres	Sidecar Tyres
L2/1 250 O.H.V. Lightweight	3·00 × 19	16	26	—
2/1 240 O.H.V. Solo	3·25 × 19	16	22	—
3/1 350 S.V. Solo	3·25 × 19	16	22	—
3/2 350 O.H.V. Solo	3·25 × 19	16	22	—
5/1 550 S.V. Sidecar	3·25 × 19	18	30	16
5/2 500 O.H.V.	3·25 × 19	18	30	16
5/5 500 O.H.V. Sports Sidecar	3·25 × 19	18	30	16
5/10 500 O.H.V.	3·00 × 21	18	30	—
Special Sports	3·25 × 21	18	22	—
6/1 650 O.H.V. Twin Sidecar	3·50 × 19	16	27	16

should be checked every week, a reliable pressure gauge being used for the purpose. The pressures shown above are the correct ones for the Dunlop tyres fitted to the various 1935-6 Triumph models.

Where a pillion passenger is carried it is usually advisable to increase the pressure of the rear tyre by 4–5 lb. per sq. in. Generally speaking, it is advisable to run the rear tyre at a moderate pressure, consistent with good steering. If the tyre is too soft the machine will tend to wander, and if too hard riding will be uncomfortable and the rear wheel will tend to bounce. The exact tyre pressures used depend upon the rider's weight and the type of machine, and are to some extent a matter for individual experiment. Below are tabulated the correct average pressures for 1937–9 solo Triumphs.

Lb. per sq. in. minimum inflation pressure		Front Tyre	Rear Tyre
Tiger 100	500 c.c. O.H.V.	22	18
Tiger 90	500 c.c. O.H.V.	22	18
Tiger 80	350 c.c. O.H.V.	20	20
Tiger 70	250 c.c. O.H.V.	18	20
Speed Twin (5T)	500 c.c. O.H.V.	22	18
Model 6S	600 c.c. S.V.	18	18
Model 5S	500 c.c. S.V.	18	18
Models 3S, 3SC	350 c.c. S.V.	16	20
Model 5H	500 c.c. O.H.V.	18	18
Model 3H	350 c.c. O.H.V.	16	20
Models 2H, 2HC	250 c.c. O.H.V.	18	20

BICYCLE PARTS

The suggested tyre pressures for 1946 Triumphs are—

	Front Tyre	Rear Tyre
De Luxe 3T	18	18
Tiger 100	20	18
Speed Twin	20	18

The improved 3T de Luxe, Speed Twin and Tiger "100" are fitted with Dunlop tyres below as standard—

	Front	Rear
3T de Luxe	3·25—19	3·25—19
Speed Twin	3·25—19	3·50—19
Tiger "100"	3·25—19	3·50—19

Triumph design wheels, 300 × 20 front, 400 × 19 rear with Dunlop Universal tyres, are used for the "Trophy" Trials model, and the tyres on the "Grand Prix" Racing model are Dunlop racing tyres 300 × 20 ribbed front, 350 × 19 triple-studded rear, fitted to Dunlop light alloy racing type rims.

The tyres should be examined regularly, particularly after riding over roads which have been tarred and gritted, and any sharp pieces of stone removed. If allowed to remain, no immediate damage may be caused, but ultimately they will work right through the cover and puncture the tube.

The Chains. The middle links of the free length of chain should move a little up and down when correctly tensioned—$\frac{1}{2}$ in. in the case of the primary chain and $\frac{3}{4}$ in. in the case of the rear chain. The chain, when new, should be adjusted two or three times during the first 500 miles, since it tends to stretch. The movement of the chains is best checked on the upper length of the primary chain and the lower length of the rear chain.

The general method for adjusting the primary chain is shown in Fig. 51. Slacken the nuts of the pivotal and clamp bolts, rotate the adjuster, after easing the locknut—clockwise to tighten the chain—and tighten support and adjuster locknuts. When the gear lever is hand-operated this adjustment may upset the adjustment of the gear control. The tension of the primary chain may be tested on oil-bath models by inserting the finger through the filler orifice, or on other models through the inspection hole covered by a detachable disc.

On 1937-9 Triumph models, access to the gear-box clamping nut is best secured by removing the off-side footrest, and pushing the spindle out of the way. It is then possible to use a spanner on the nut satisfactorily. It should be particularly noted that failure to slacken the clamping nut when making chain tension

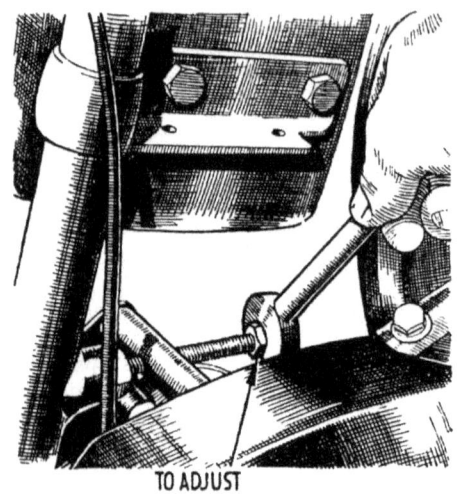

TO ADJUST
PRIMARY CHAIN

Fig. 51. Showing How to Adjust Primary Chain

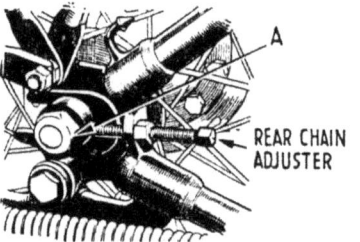

Fig. 51A. Showing Rear Chain Adjuster

adjustment will result in a fractured gear-box casing. Access to the gear-box trunnion bolt is obtained from beneath the machine, between the mudguard and gear-box.

The primary drive on Model 6/1 requires no adjustment, because it consists of two double helical gear wheels.

When adjusting the rear chain great care should be exercised not to interfere with the alignment; it is essential to adjust each side of the axle equally. This is, however, quite a simple operation. All that is necessary is to slacken the outside axle nuts (A, Fig. 51A) and the locknuts on the adjusters, rotate the latter in a clockwise direction to tighten, moving each one the same number of turns, finally securing all the nuts. Adjusting the tension of the rear chain affects the adjustment of the brake, so readers are referred to page 85.

Slack or badly adjusted chains are a frequent cause of harsh and excessive wear. On the 1946-9 models, the adjustment to both should allow ½ in. free up and down movement midway between the sprockets. The gear-box and back wheel clamping nuts must be kept tight and both chains well lubricated.

The best way of getting at the gear-box clamping nut is to remove the off-side footrest and push the spindle out of the way. The spanner can then be got on to the nut and adequate purchase secured. The gear-box casing is liable to be fractured if the clamping nut is not slackened off. Access to the gear-box trunnion bolt is obtained from beneath the machine, between the mudguard

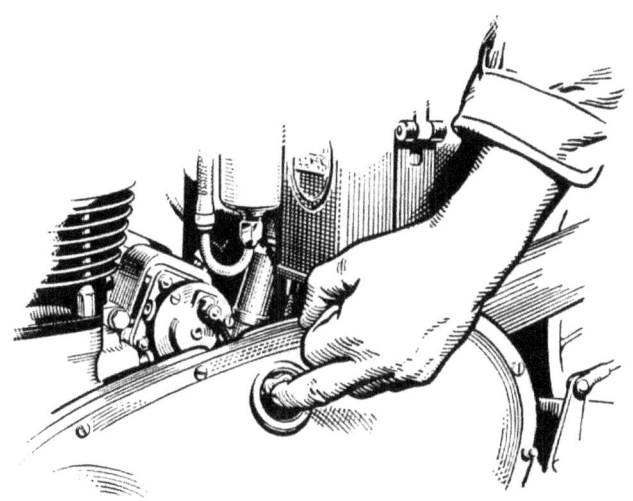

Fig. 52. Checking the Adjustment of the Primary Chain (1946 Models)

and the gear-box. The quantity of oil fed to the rear chain is governed by an adjusting screw situated at the back of the primary chain case. Trial and error adjustment is advisable to arrive at correct rear chain lubrication. It is a good plan to close the adjusting screw completely, after which it should be unscrewed two and a half turns.

Modern chains give a very large mileage, if properly serviced, but the result of abuse is noticeable more quickly than in any other component of the machine. For the sake of economy, the rider is advised to carry out maintenance duties regularly.

Every 1500 miles in summer, and every 1000 miles in winter, the rear chain should be removed and cleaned. This can be done most efficiently by giving it successive baths in clean paraffin; a number is usually necessary before the chain is quite clean and free from grit. It should be allowed to remain in a bath of molten graphite grease until it has cooled off and the grease is solid again. This allows the grease to penetrate underneath the rollers.

When the chain is removed, surplus grease should be wiped off, and the chain refitted and adjusted. Care should be taken to see that the spring fastener on the removable link is replaced in the right position. The spring fastener is roughly shaped like a fish—the nose should proceed in a forward direction when the machine is running, as a fish swims nose first.

Chain Alterations and Repairs. In the event of it being necessary to repair, lengthen or shorten a chain a rivet extractor and

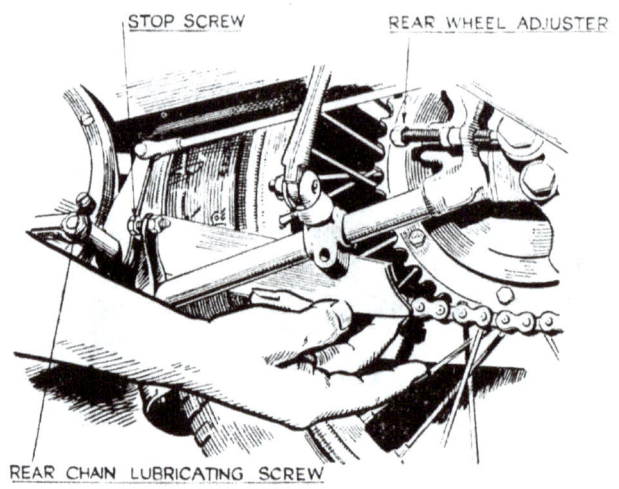

Fig. 53. Checking the Adjustment of the Rear Chain

a few spare parts will be required. The rivet extractor is suitable for chains up to ¾ in. pitch, whether they are on or off the wheels. It should be used in the following manner: First turn the screw anti-clockwise to allow the punch end to clear the chain rivet, then open the jaws by gripping the tommy bar and handle together, as shown No. 1, Fig. 54, pass the jaws over the chain and release the grip. As will be seen in No. 2, Fig. 54, the jaws should rest on a chain roller free of chain link plates. Finally, turn the screw clockwise until the punch contacts with and pushes out rivet end through the chain outer link plate. Unscrew the punch, withdraw extractor, and repeat the whole operation on the adjacent rivet in the same chain outer link plate. The outer plate is then free and the two rivets can be withdrawn from the opposite side with the opposite plate in position. The removed part should not be used again.

If the chain has a broken roller or inside link, it can be repaired by removing the dark parts in No. 5, Fig. 55, and replacing by two single connecting links and one inner link as shown in No. 6.

When a chain has to be shortened, the exact procedure depends upon whether it contains an even or an odd number of pitches. In the former case, remove the dark parts No. 1, Fig. 55, and replace by cranked double link and single connecting link, as No. 2. In the latter case, remove the dark parts shown in No. 3, Fig. 55, and replace by single connecting link and inner link, No. 4.

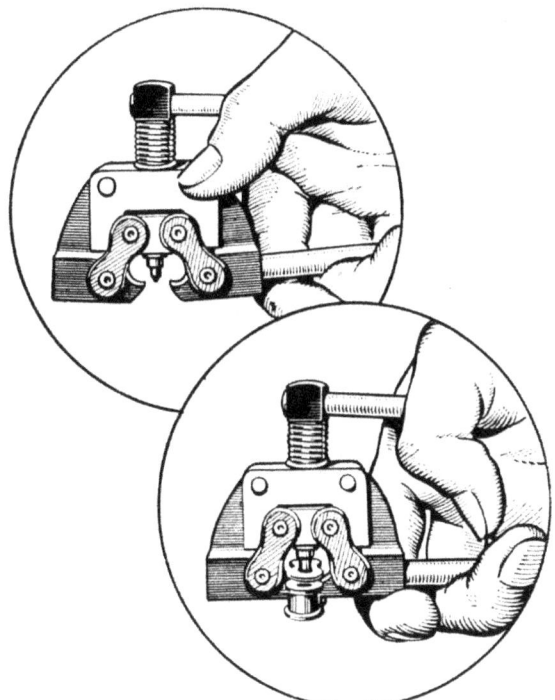

FIG. 54. THE CHAIN RIVET EXTRACTOR

Brake Adjustment (1935-6). The adjustment of the brakes on each wheel is by means of the knurled nut nearest the end of the rod. This should be rotated in a clockwise direction to take up control slack or to compensate for lining wear. Both brakes should be set so that the shoes begin to contact when the lever has covered approximately one-fifth of its total travel, making sure that the wheel is free in the " off " position. When inter-connected brakes are fitted, the wheels should be adjusted individually, as above; and then operate the sleeve adjustment at the foot brake pedal extremity of the connecting cable; this causes the application of the rear brake to begin slightly in front of the front brake.

86   THE BOOK OF THE TRIUMPH

The adjustment of the foot pedal stop determines the height of the pedal, so its operation should be carried out in collaboration with the foregoing.

Brake Adjustment (1937-9). Two separate adjustments are provided for the front brake. Normally adjustment should be

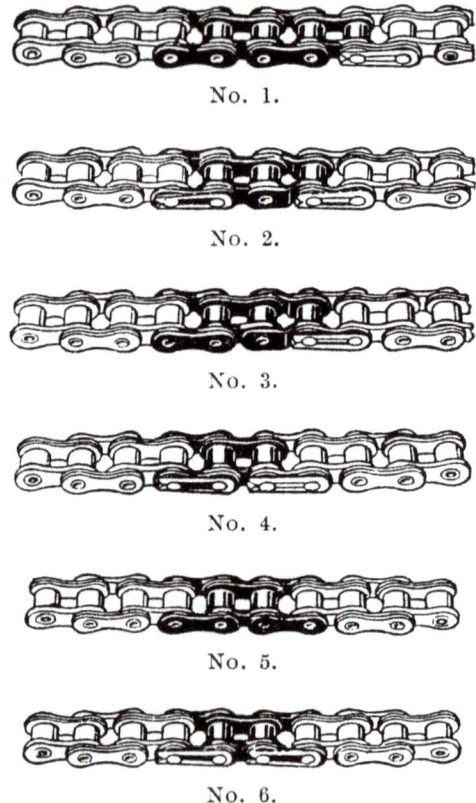

Fig. 55. Chain Repairs

made by means of the finger-operated adjuster on the forks just in front of the shock-absorber. The adjustment should be such that when the brake is full on the hand lever it is just clear of the handlebars. This enables the rider to exert maximum pressure with his hand. There is in addition to the above adjustment a clevis at the foot of the rod where it is attached to the cam spindle lever. To adjust the clevis, remove the pin and loosen the locknut, the clevis may then be screwed farther along the

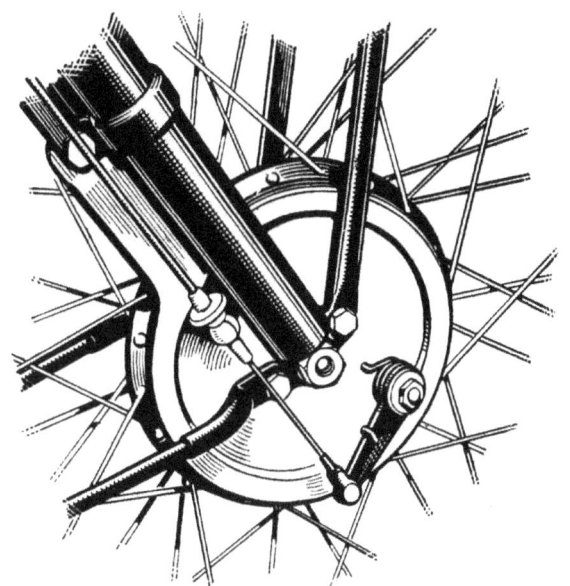

Fig. 56. Front Brake Adjustment

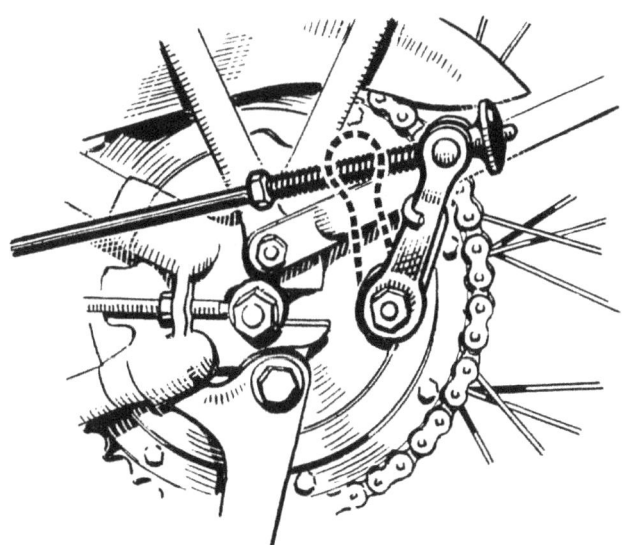

Fig. 57. Rear Brake Adjustment

rod in order to compensate for wear of the brake shoe linings. The second adjustment, however, should be made only when the first adjustment is found insufficient.

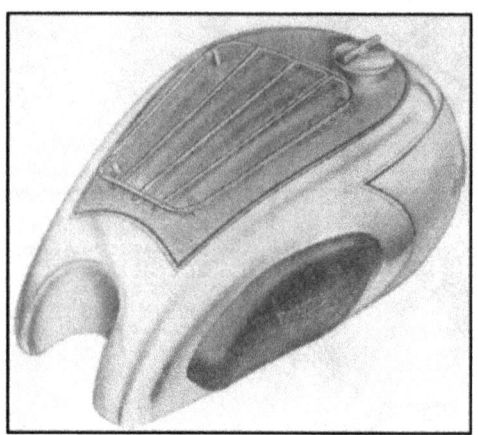

FIG. 58. PARCEL GRID

Finger adjustment is also provided on the end of the rear brake rod and adjustment should be such that the brake shoes are just clear of the brake drum when the brake pedal is released. This enables slight toe pressure to exert powerful retardation, a factor which makes for safety, especially when the roads are treacherous. A brake pedal stop (see page 2) is provided, and this should be adjusted to suit the rider *before* adjusting the effective length of the brake rod. After adjusting either brake, test for free running of the wheel. Brakes which bind absorb power and cause the shoe linings to wear quickly.

When the brakes are new they are never fully efficient; they must be given time to bed down properly. On the 1946-9 Triumphs there is a knurled finger adjuster on the brake anchor plate for adjusting the front brake. The correct setting is for the lever to be just clear of the handlebar when the brake is fully applied. The maximum amount of grip can be exerted under such conditions. The adjustment of the rear brake is shown in Fig. 57. The position of the brake lever, as shown with the brake off, denotes that the lining is in good order; the dotted line indicates the position of the lever when the linings are badly worn.

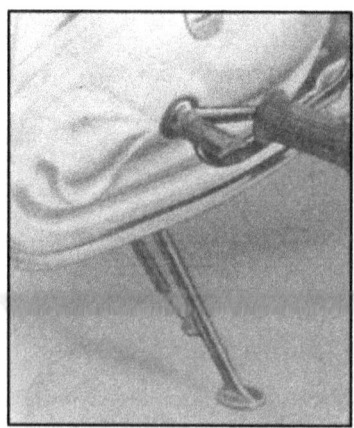

FIG. 59. PROP STAND

Petrol Tank Grid. The parcel grid is an extra fitment to the 3T de Luxe, Speed Twin and Tiger " 100 " models, and has been designed to bolt on the top of the petrol tank. This chromium-plated grid, to which small parcels may be attached, is particularly useful to the long-distance solo rider. When the grid is not in use, rubber plugs are fitted into the four threaded holes (Fig. 58).

Prop Stand. This is available as an extra on all models. It attaches to the nearside cradle member of the frame. A spring retains the stand out as a prop or in the folded back position. It can be fitted to all Triumph models from 1937 (Fig. 59).

The Sidecar. With straight edges placed alongside the machine and car wheels, the lateral adjustment should provide that the dimension immediately ahead of the front wheel, line $A-C$,

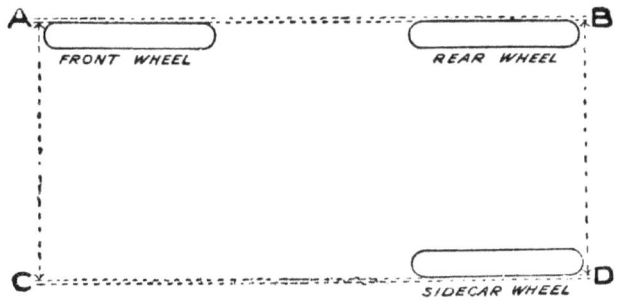

Fig. 60. How to Align the Sidecar

is $\frac{3}{8}$ in. less than behind the rear wheels, line $B-D$, as shown in Fig. 60. The telescopic arms should be adjusted so that the machine leans slightly out of the vertical to the off-side.

To maintain the sidecar in good running order the spring bearing nipples should be greased frequently, while periodically the leaves should be separated and a little grease inserted. The wheel should be tested for play. Play can be taken up by removing the outer cap and the split pin, and then easing the castellated nut back a few turns and rotating the adjusting cone, as necessary.

CHAPTER VII
MECHANICAL ADJUSTMENTS

THE likelihood of the need for extensive and costly repairs developing is lessened considerably by periodic adjustment. Intelligent anticipation of trouble is advantageous, but constant tinkering and tampering is inadvisable. The following paragraphs should be read carefully and always referred to if in doubt before any adjustment is to be undertaken.

Tappet Adjustment (1935-6 S.V. and O.H.V. Models). The clearance should be tested and adjusted when the engine is cold and

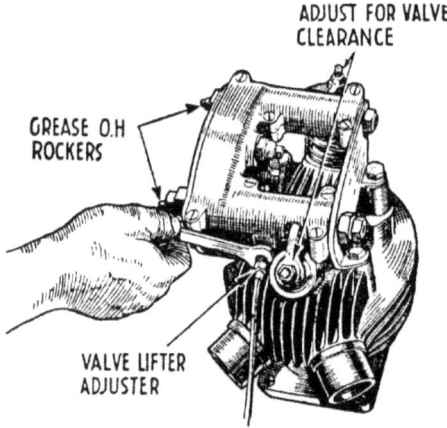

FIG. 61. ADJUSTING TAPPET CLEARANCES (MODELS 5/2, 5/5, 6/1)

with both valves closed. It is a simple operation, but it should be carried out carefully. The principle for Models 5/2, 5/5 and 6/1 is shown in Fig. 61; slacken the locknuts on the rocker, tighten the adjusting screw to give clearance below, and tighten the locknut. A feeler gauge should always be employed. In the case of Models 3/1 and 5/1 the valve chest covers should be removed; after slackening the locknut, the tappet head should be turned as necessary to give the desired clearance, and the locknut should be secured.

A different plan must be followed on Models L2/1, 2/1 and 3/2. These O.H.V. engines are adjusted as follows: slacken the large hexagon nut at the base of the push rod cover tube and, when clear of the guide threads, slide forward, telescoping the tube into the upper half; then engage one spanner with the hexagon nut on the tappet top and a second spanner on the locknut-release, and rotate the top until easy rotation of the rod is just possible, then secure. It may be mentioned that a feeler gauge cannot be used for checking the clearance on these models, but the plan outlined gives correct results.

The correct clearances on Models 5/2, 5/5 and 6/1 are 0·002 in. for the exhaust valve and 0·0015 in. for the inlet valve; on

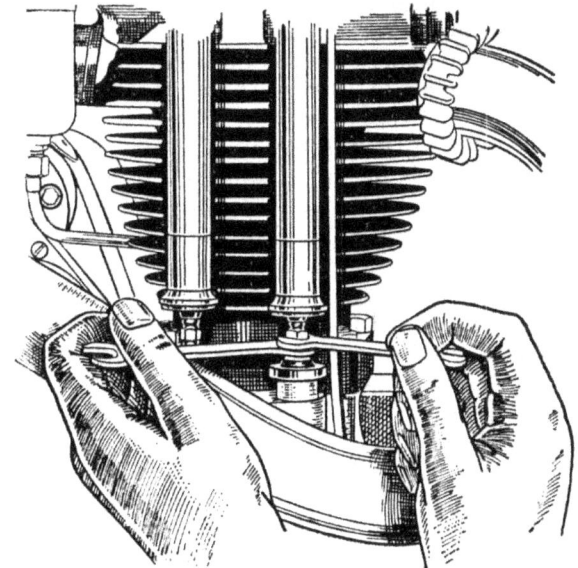

FIG. 62. ADJUSTING THE TAPPETS (1937-9 O.H.V. SINGLES)

Models 3/1 and 5/1, 0·004 in. for the exhaust valve and 0·003 in. for the inlet valve.

Adjust the oil flow to the rockers and rear cylinder respectively in small stages in the case of Models L2/1, 2/1, 3/2, and 5/10.

Tappet Adjustment (1937-9 S.V. and O.H.V. Models). On all engines the tappets should be adjusted with the engine quite *cold*. To adjust the tappets on the single-cylinder O.H.V. models, proceed as follows. First raise the push rod cover tubes so as to expose the tappets. This may be done with a screwdriver, and a distance piece (supplied in the tool kit) may be employed to prop up the cover tubes while the tappets are being attended to. It is important to see that neither push rod cover tube springs back into its cup, otherwise the latter may suffer damage. To make the actual adjustment, rotate the engine gently with the kick-starter until the inlet tappet has just moved downwards and continue rotation a little further until engine compression is felt. Then loosen the tappet locknut with one spanner and with another turn the adjustable tappet head as shown in Fig. 62, until there is no up and down play but the push rod is able to revolve freely. This is the correct adjustment.

Now retighten the locknut while preventing the tappet head from moving. Afterwards again check the tappet adjustment. Deal with the inlet and exhaust tappets similarly. Finally ease the push rod cover tubes very carefully down on to their cups.

The method of adjusting the tappets on the side-valve engines is similar to that described above, but as the valve stems, instead of push rods, make contact with the tappet heads, the tappet clearances may be checked with a feeler gauge. The correct clearances are 0·004 in. and 0·007 in. for the inlet and exhaust tappets respectively. In order to gain access to the tappets, take off the valve chest cover. Be careful with the washer.

In the case of the twin-cylinder engines, rocker arm adjuster screws are used for valve clearance adjustment. First remove the four caps on the rocker boxes so as to expose the adjusters. Then turn the engine over until the piston in the cylinder being dealt with is at T.D.C. on the compression stroke, with both valves fully closed. Now slacken off the locknut with the hexagonal ring spanner (supplied in the tool kit) and turn the squared end of the adjuster on each rocker arm with the special spanner provided until there is just the faintest up and down "shake" on the rocker arm—equivalent to a clearance of about 0·001 in. Retighten the locknuts, again check the adjustment, and replace the rocker box caps. Having dealt with one cylinder, deal with the other one similarly. Finally test the engine compression to make sure that all four valves are seating properly.

The Exhaust Valve Lifter. The exhaust valve must seat properly, but the lifter should be adjusted in such a way that it comes into action very soon after movement of the lever begins. Care should be taken not to adjust too closely on O.H.V. engines, or a tapping noise will result. The clearance by the sleeve nut at the abutment on the rocker box, for O.H.V. engines (this is on the front tank support lug in the case of Model L2/1) and the side of the valve chest on side-valve models should be adjusted.

On the 1946-9 models tappet adjustment is made on the rocker arms after removing the four tappet inspection caps in the case of the 500 c.c., and the two tappet inspection covers on the 350 c.c. rocker boxes. The cylinder concerned must be on the compression stroke; this can be determined by watching the inlet rocker arm to see that the valve closes, then the kick-starter should be re pressed a little farther to bring the piston against compression.

MECHANICAL ADJUSTMENTS

To adjust, slacken off the locknut with the hexagonal ring spanner, then turn the squared end of the tappet adjusting pin with the special spanner provided. A clearance of about 1 thou. is desirable; this means there is just a very slight amount of up and down shake on the rocker arm. The compression should always be tested after adjusting the tappets, so as to make sure the valves are seating properly. The method of adjusting the tappets is

FIG. 63. METHOD OF TAPPET ADJUSTMENT (1946-9 MODELS)

shown in Fig. 63. The adjustment of the tappets should always be done when the engine is cold.

The Clutch. To allow the clutch to function correctly there should be a free movement of $\frac{3}{16}$ in. on the cable. This can be maintained by adjustment at the screwed abutment on the gear-box inner cover. Slacken the locknut and screw the sleeve clockwise to remove play, securing the locknut afterwards. A further adjustment is provided. This is to take up wear on the clutch push rod and is to be found on the lever (1935-6). This is supplementary to the cable adjustment and is carried out by easing the locknut securing screw which forms the grease nipple and rotating the latter, as necessary. The clutch should be adjusted two or three times during the first 500 miles, as the plates bed down.

On 1937-9 models the supplementary clutch adjustment comprises a screw and locknut situated underneath the gear-box filler cap where it is readily accessible and entirely enclosed. It is important always to maintain a slight amount of play between the clutch arm and the push rod which operates the clutch. Triumph clutches have four springs arranged radially on the outer clutch plate and the tension of these springs should be adjusted only sufficiently to prevent slip. Excessive tightening of the screws will cause clutch drag, and difficulty in engaging first gear from neutral. On all 1937-9 models the clutch is enclosed in the primary oil-bath and runs immersed in oil. Therefore see that there is ¾ pint of *suitable* oil (page 36) in the chain case, otherwise clutch drag may develop. Should the clutch plates be removed, it is necessary to oil the plates before reassembly by dipping into a bath of oil.

To adjust spring tension (1935-6), when an oil bath is employed, detach the brake coupling wire, if used, the footrest and the cover screws, but only after draining out the oil. It should be remembered that when refitting all the old sealing compound should be removed, and then the joint should be smeared with shellac or gold size before replacing; the screws must be tightened evenly and fully.

A steel cover is used on Models L2/1, 3/1 and 5/1. On these machines detach the footrest, the outer nut and brake pedal from the shaft and the fixing screws from the flange, then the cover can be removed.

In the case of ferodo-lined 6-spring clutches, mainly on Models L2/1 and 3/1, there is no adjustment for spring tension, for it is essential for the stud nuts to be screwed home.

A cork-lined clutch, with spring pressure adjustable at four points, is fitted on Models 2/1, 3/2, 5/1, 5/2, 5/5 and 6/1. This type of clutch can be adjusted by easing the outer of the two nuts on each stud and rotating the inner nut to give the required tension, but it is essential to see that all four are treated equally, so that the clutch withdraws evenly over the whole area. The position of the inner nuts should be retained while the locknuts are being tightened.

On the 1946-9 models the clutch consists of a series of steel plates provided with cork inserts, between which plain steel plates are fitted. There are certain precautions which the rider should adopt if the cork inserts are to give long and trouble-free service. Always engage the neutral position when the machine is stationary. Never stop the machine in traffic by extracting the clutch; excepting when changing gear or getting into neutral the clutch should be fully engaged. Never slip the clutch on corners or to avoid changing down.

The clutch control cable passes through the lug on the outside of the gear-box inner cover, and is there provided with an adjustment. Immediately underneath the gear-box filler cap there is

MECHANICAL ADJUSTMENTS

also an adjustment for the clutch operating rod; this is readily accessible, although it is enclosed. There should be only a slight amount of free movement between the clutch arm and the clutch operating rod; this is secured by means of the adjuster inside the gear-box filler cap. The length of cable is adjusted by means of the cable adjuster on the gear-box lug. So as to ensure the clutch being fully engaged when the handlebar lever is released, there should be a slight amount of free movement at the handlebar end.

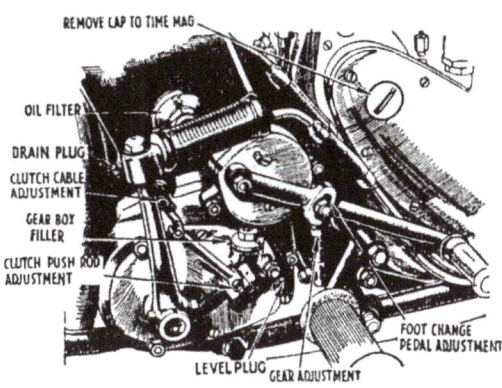

FIG. 64. GEAR-BOX ADJUSTMENT (1935-6)

Four springs are employed to hold the clutch plates together; they are accessible after removing the primary chain case. These springs are tensioned by four screws which should be sufficiently tightened to prevent the clutch slipping; a special key is provided in the tool kit. Excessive tightening prevents the clutch freeing properly.

Gear-box and Controls. As previously mentioned, it is necessary to re-set the gear control after the chain has been adjusted. This is, however, only in the case of a hand-operated control and it does not apply when foot control is fitted. Re-setting is best done as follows: Slacken the locknut at the top and bottom of the

FIG. 65. BROKEN-OPEN VIEW OF 1946 GEAR-BOX

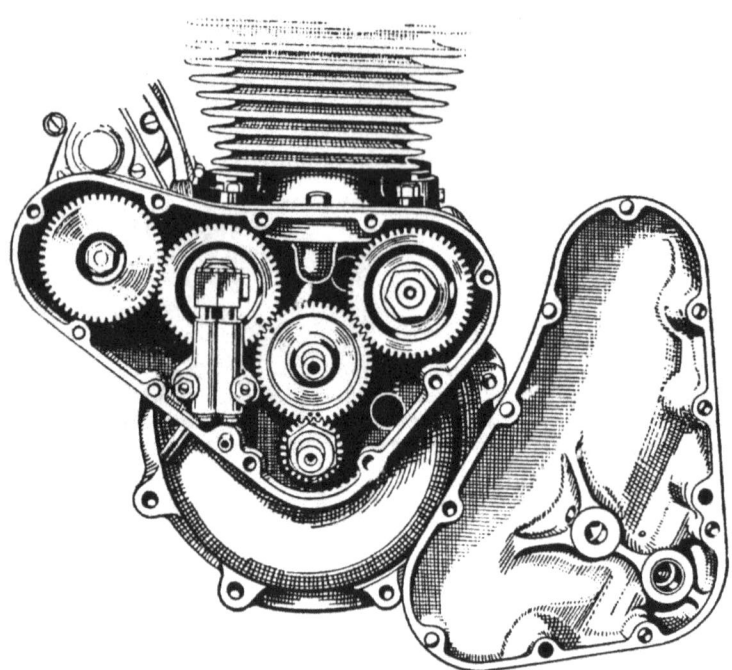

Fig. 66. Timing Gear (Twin-cylinder Triumph)
Note the dot system of marking the timing gears which makes correct replacement very simple

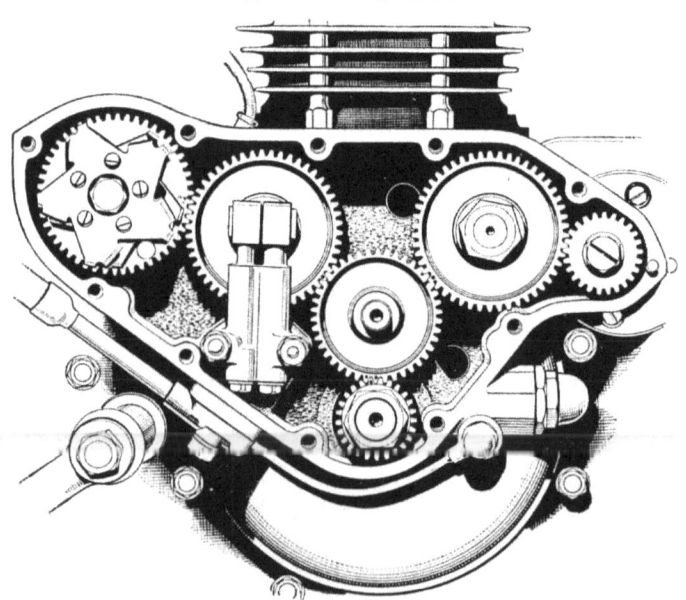

Fig. 67. Timing Gear (1946–9 Models)

MECHANICAL ADJUSTMENTS 97

vertical operating rod, remove the ball pin nut, and withdraw the top end from the hand lever; ensure location of second gear in the box and position the hand lever to suit. Offer up the top ball pin to the lever, rotating the rod to right or left, to give easy entry to the lever hole. The rod is threaded right- and left-hand at the ball pin connexions; rotate as necessary to elongate or contract. Tighten all nuts.

The gear-box of the 1946-9 Triumphs requires no attention, with the exception of regular changing of the lubricant. Reference to Fig. 65 shows clearly the general arrangement of the gear selection mechanism. When the gear change pedal is operated one or other of the cam faced plungers is depressed against its spring as it is forced into contact with the plunger plate.

Valve Timing. The general arrangement of the timing gear of the 1935-9 Triumphs is shown in Figs. 12 and 66, and of the 1946-9 models in Fig. 67. It is impossible to time the engine incorrectly, as the teeth which are meshed together in the timing gears are punch marked.

IGNITION TIMING

The Four-stroke Timing Gear. The general arrangement of the timing gear is shown in Figs. 12, 66. Punch marks are impressed adjacent to the teeth to serve as a guide when refitting, and to enable the motor-cyclist to restore the valve timing correctly. The valve timing on the various 1935-6 models is as follows—

1935-6 VALVE TIMINGS*

	L2/1 Deg. MM.	2/1 Deg. MM.	3/1 Deg. MM.
Inlet opens BTC	17 or 2	36 or 9	15 or 2·25
Inlet closes ABC	53 ,, 13·75	70 ,, 22	53 ,, 13·75
Exhaust opens BBC	64 ,, 18	70 ,, 22	65 ,, 20·5
Exhaust closes ATC	26 ,, 5	36 ,, 9	21 ,, 4·25
	3/2 Deg. MM.	5/1 Deg. MM.	5/2 Deg. MM.
Inlet opens BTC	36 or 10·25	15 or 2·25	36 or 10·25
Inlet closes ABC	70 ,, 24·5	53 ,, 15·75	70 ,, 24·5
Exhaust opens BBC	70 ,, 24·5	65 ,, 23·25	70 ,, 24·5
Exhaust closes ATC	36 ,, 10·25	21 ,, 4·25	36 ,, 10·25
	5/5 Deg. MM.	5/10 Deg. MM.	6/1 Deg. MM.
Inlet opens BTC	40 or 12·75	30 or 7·5	24 or 4·5
Inlet closes ABC	70 ,, 24·5	64 ,, 20·75	60 ,, 16·75
Exhaust opens BBC	70 ,, 24·5	64 ,, 20·75	70 ,, 23·25
Exhaust closes ATC	40 ,, 12·75	30 ,, 7·5	28 ,, 6·25

* All valve timings given should be checked with *nil* valve clearances. This is important.

It will be noticed that the inlet valve opens *before* top centre and closes *after* bottom centre, while the exhaust valve opens *before* bottom centre and closes *after* top centre.

The correct valve timing for the various 1937-9 Triumph models will be found tabulated below.

1937-8 Valve Timings*

	5T (Twin) Deg. MM.	T90 Deg. MM.	T80 Deg. MM.
Inlet opens BTC	21 or 3·25	25 or 5	36 or 10·25
Inlet closes ABT	75 ,, 25	80 ,, 41·75	70 ,, 24·5
Exhaust opens BBC	75 ,, 25	80 ,, 31·5	70 ,, 24·5
Exhaust closes ATC	21 ,, 3·25	36 ,, 10·25	36 ,, 10·25

	T70 Deg. MM.	6S Deg. MM.	5H Deg. MM.
Inlet opens BTC	36 or 9	15 or 2·25	25 or 5
Inlet closes ABT	70 ,, 22	53 ,, 13·75	80 ,, 41·75
Exhaust opens BBC	70 ,, 22	65 ,, 20·5	80 ,, 31·5
Exhaust closes ATC	36 ,, 9	21 ,, 4·25	36 ,, 10·25

	3H Deg. MM.	3S, 3SC Deg. MM.	2H, 2HC Deg. MM.
Inlet opens BTC	36 or 10·25	15 or 2·25	36 or 9
Inlet closes ABT	70 ,, 24·5	53 ,, 13·75	70 ,, 22
Exhaust opens BBC	70 ,, 24·5	65 ,, 20·5	70 ,, 22
Exhaust closes ATC	36 ,, 10·25	21 ,, 4·25	36 ,, 9

1939 Valve Timings*

	5T (Twin)	T100	T70, T80
Inlet opens BTC	26·5 degrees	26·5 degrees	36 degrees
Inlet closes ABC	69·5 ,,	69 ,,	70 ,,
Exhaust opens BBC	61 ,,	61 ,,	70 ,,
Exhaust closes ATC	35 ,,	35 ,,	36 ,,

	6S	5H	5S
Inlet opens BTC	19 degrees	26·5 degrees	19 degrees
Inlet closes ABC	60 ,,	62·5 ,,	60 ,,
Exhaust opens BBC	67 ,,	75·5 ,,	67 ,,
Exhaust closes ATC	29 ,,	20·5 ,,	29 ,,

	3H	3S	2H, 2HC
Inlet opens BTC	36 degrees	19 degrees	36 degrees
Inlet closes ABC	70 ,,	60 ,,	70 ,,
Exhaust opens BBC	70 ,,	67 ,,	70 ,,
Exhaust closes ATC	29 ,,	36 ,,	36 ,,

To Retime the "Magdyno." Correct ignition timing gives maximum all-round performance and subjects the engine bearings to the least strain. On all Triumph machines the "Magdyno" is

* All valve timings given should be checked with *nil* valve clearances. This is important.

MECHANICAL ADJUSTMENTS

gear driven (Figs. 12, 66) and to retime the ignition proceed as follows. First turn the engine over gently until the piston is at the top of the *compression* stroke with both valves closed. Then remove the sparking plug and find the exact top dead centre (T.D.C.) position of the piston by rocking the engine to and fro and noting the position where a piece of wire inserted through the plug hole does not move. Mark the wire where it touches the top of the plug hole and remove the wire and scratch another mark $\frac{5}{16}$ in., as the case may be, above the first one. Now replace the wire and turn the engine over until the upper mark takes the place of the first one. The piston will then have descended $\frac{5}{16}$ in. (or whatever is the correct advance). In this position the contacts of the contact breaker should commence to "break." If they do not do so, remove the timing cover and loosen the "Magdyno" driving pinion from the spindle taper. To do this on the twin-cylinder engines a pinion extractor (provided in the tool kit) must be used. In the case of the single-cylinder engines a special extractor nut is used for securing and removing the driving pinion. By unscrewing the nut a few turns the pinion is released. Further unscrewing will remove it completely from the tapered spindle. Unscrew the nut with care and progressively, otherwise the three rivets may be pulled. Having loosened the pinion, turn the armature until the contacts are just "breaking," secure the pinion firmly without moving the armature or piston (which should be in the position described above), again check the timing, and finally replace the timing cover.

1935-9 Ignition Timings. On all models the ignition lever should be set in the *fully advanced* position. The position of the piston before top dead centre should be as follows: on Models L2/1, 2/1, 3/1, 5/1, and on 1937-8 Models 6S, 3S, 3SC, 2H, 2HC —$\frac{11}{32}$ in. before T.D.C.; on the 1935-6 Model 3/2, the 1937-8 Models T100, T80, T70, 5H, 3H, 5T, and the 1939 Models 2H, 2HC —$\frac{3}{8}$ in. before the T.D.C.; on the 1937-8 Model T90—$\frac{13}{32}$ in. before T.D.C.; on the 1939 Models 6S, 5S, 3S, 3SC—$\frac{5}{16}$ in. before T.D.C.

Ignition Timing (1946 Triumphs). A depth gauge should be used when timing the ignition; this can be made from a piece of spoke about 5 in. long, graduated in sixteenths of an inch with a small fine file. With magneto fully advanced and contact breaker points just breaking, ignition on the 350 c.c. and 500 c.c. machines is correctly timed when the off-side piston is—

350 c.c.	.	.	.	.	$\frac{11}{32}$ in. BTDC*
500 c.c.			.	.	$\frac{3}{8}$ in. BTDC

* $\frac{9}{32}$ in. with low octane fuel.

100   THE BOOK OF THE TRIUMPH

To time the magneto in the fully advanced position, the automatic control must be wedged, as shown in Fig. 68. This is done by turning the mechanism in an anti-clockwise direction, against the spring, and inserting the tool kit screwdriver between one of the bob-weights and the retard control lip. Make certain the mechanism is touching the fully advanced stop when the screwdriver is in position. Take off the contact breaker cover and turn the magneto in the direction of rotation (anti-clockwise, as viewed from the drive end) until the contact points are just opening with the points as shown in Fig. 69. Take out a sparking plug and turn the engine by engaging a gear and, with the machine on the stand, rotate the rear wheel in the direction for forward travel. Turn until both off-side valves are closed on the compression stroke, then bring the off-side piston to T.D.C. and insert the gauge through the plug hole to test the position. Make sure

Fig. 68. Auto Advance (1946–9 Models)

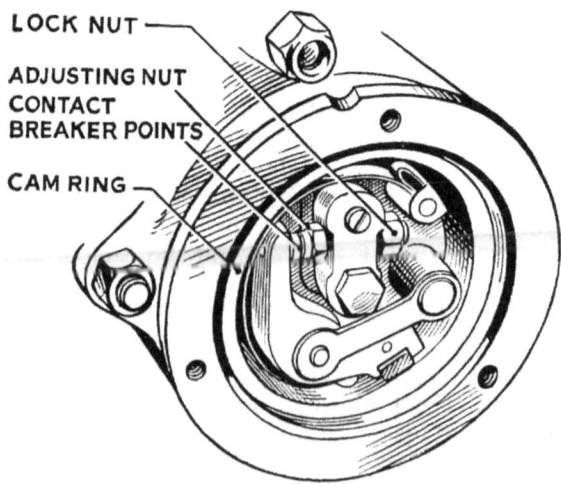

Fig. 69. Contact Breaker (1946–9 Models)

the engine is on true T.D.C., then rotate the engine backwards until the piston has dropped $\frac{11}{32}$ in. or $\frac{3}{8}$ in., as the case may be. Check up to see the magneto is correctly positioned with the points just breaking, then tighten up the nut carefully on the armature shaft until a grip is felt. Release the screwdriver immediately; otherwise serious damage will be done. After removing the screwdriver tighten up the shaft nut. Lastly, turn the engine over a

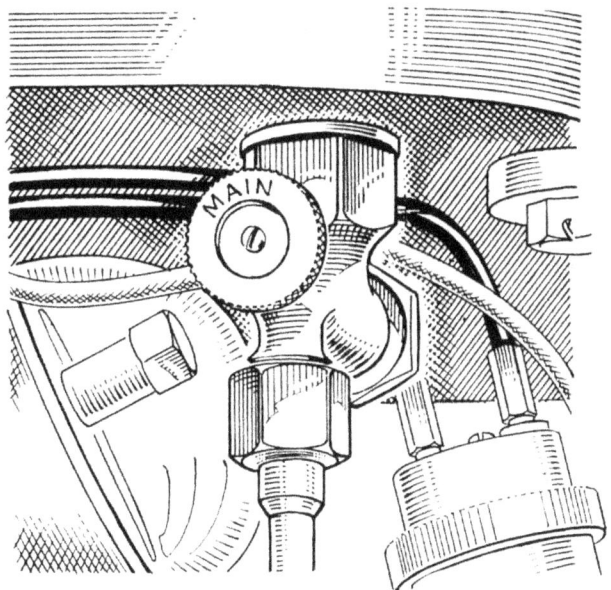

FIG. 70. PETROL TAP

few times, then make a final check by positioning the piston again at the correct measurement before T.D.C., and seeing that the contact breaker points are just opening in the fully advanced position.

Petrol Tap Adjustment. Adjust the petrol tap if it should leak. This can be done by first slacking off the locking screw in the tap body and then withdrawing the plunger assembly. Grip the plunger end and turn the plunger knob in a clockwise direction, so as to expand the cork washer and make a tighter fit.

CHAPTER VIII

OVERHAULING: DISMANTLING AND RE-ASSEMBLY PROCEDURE

THE average motor-cyclist is strongly advised to leave major overhauling to an experienced mechanic since, as a rule, he is not capable of dismantling some of the units successfully. There are certain tasks, however, which may be undertaken and these are discussed in the following pages.

General Hints (1935-6). If there is any chance of interfering with the electrical equipment when carrying out any major job, the positive battery lead should be disconnected at the sleeve connexion.

If the upper part of the engine has to be attended to it makes the work more easy if the petrol tank is removed in the case of the O.H.V. models. This can be done in the following manner: Remove the fuel and oil indicator tubes; take off the panel equipment, if fitted, by removing the four screws, noting the sealing beading, and secure to the handlebars—this can be done without fear of a shock if the positive battery lead has been severed, as suggested; detach the gear control quadrant, if hand-operated; take out the support bolts and, in some instances, the saddle peak bolt and cover strap. On Model 5/10 release the steering damper anchorage. The tank, by the way, need not be drained before removal. In the case of Model 6/1 it is also better if the steering damper knob is removed, for this allows the handle-bar —after easing the clip bolts—to be swung upwards and forwards.

Dismantling (1935-6). The following is the suggested order of dismantling with Models L2/1, 2/1 and 3/2 (Fig. 71): Tank, as previously described; torque stay; detach exhaust lifter wire nipple from the lever; rocker oil feed (O/S) and return (N/S) pipes; loosen the top and bottom halves of the push rod cover tubes and partially telescope to reveal the extremities of the push rods; remove the two horizontal bolts on the off-side and the two nuts from the top cylinder stud on the rear side, so as to free the rocker unit; detach the carburettor and exhaust pipe; take out the four cylinder head bolts, so as to free the casting with the valves still in position; and, if conditions warrant, the barrel can also be withdrawn at this stage, although this is not necessary on each occasion when the cylinder head and piston crown are cleaned.

OVERHAULING 103

Models 5/2, 5/5, and 5/10. Remove the tank; the two torque stays; the inlet valve oil feed pipe; the two horizontal bolts

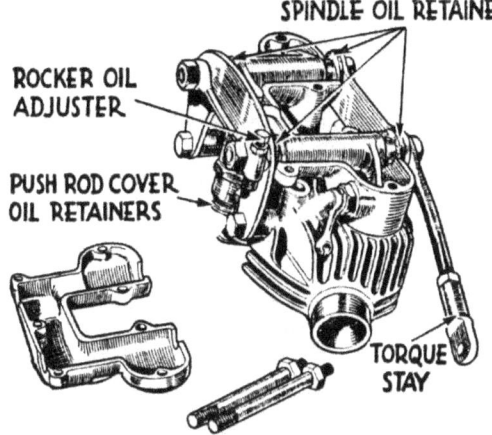

Fig. 71. Rocker Gear Details (L2/1, 2/1, 3/2)

(O/S) and the two vertical bolts (N/S), so freeing the rocker box, then detach the exhaust lifter wire—the push rod covers are a

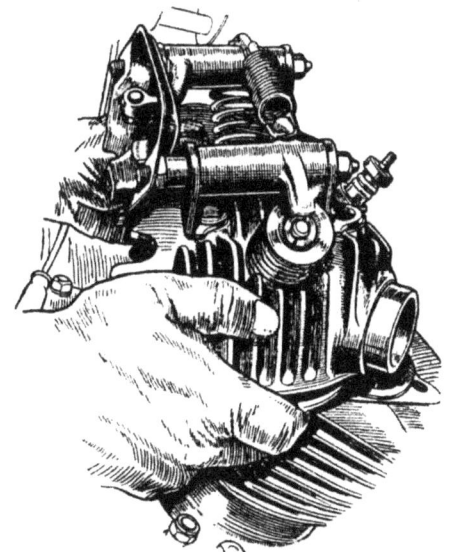

Fig. 72. Cylinder Head Removal (Early O.H.V.)

push fit in aluminium; carburettor; exhaust pipes; the remaining cylinder head bolts—one at the front of the cylinder, removing downwards; lift head clear (Fig. 72); unscrew the push rod covers and remove with the tubes; remove base nuts—four—if the barrel is to be removed; and in the case of Model 5/10 there is an extra oil pipe to the rear of the barrel.

With Models 3/1 and 5/1, remove the torque stay; the cylinder head bolts; the cylinder head (Fig. 73); and, if the removal of the barrel is necessary, the carburettor, the valve cover and washer, the exhaust lifter, the silencer pipe and the base nuts.

Model 6/1 differs from the foregoing and should be dismantled as follows: Remove the tank; the two torque stays; the exhaust

FIG. 73. REMOVAL OF CYLINDER (EARLY S.V.)

pipes; the detachable lower tank rail; secure wires to the top tube; remove the four bolts releasing the rocker box; detach the exhaust lifter wire; remove the carburettor and induction pipe; the oil feed pipes to the inlet valve guides; withdraw the push rods and cover tubes, marking them in some way, so that they will be returned to the same position—the exhaust ones are slightly longer; the cylinder head bolts—two above and two beneath each; the heads with the valves; and to release the cylinder block, remove the eight base nuts.

Valve Removal (1935-6). The cylinder head should be placed on to a flat surface with a wooden block, roughly following the shape of the combustion chamber, inside. The object of this is to prevent the valve head moving when pressure is applied to the spring collars to release the collets, cups and springs. Pressing on the collars, poke the collets out of their recesses with a small screwdriver, refitting by reversing the process.

Piston Removal. The circlip must be dislodged if the gudgeon-pin is to be detached (Fig. 74). A fairly sharp instrument should

OVERHAULING

be used for this, such as the tang end of a file; it should be inserted in the slot below the main orifice and levered to bring the clip out of its seating. Before replacing, see that the circlip has not lost its tension; it must grip the groove tightly.

The piston rings should not require removal from their grooves more frequently than every 8000 miles, unless it happens that there are signs of excessive carbon deposit in the grooves. The rings can best be removed with strips of metal about $1\frac{1}{2}$ in. long and $\frac{3}{8}$ in. wide.

1935-6 Rocker Gear. As a general rule, it is possible to treat the rocker gear on Models L2/1, 2/1, and 3/2 (Fig. 71) as a unit, returning it as such after the joint surfaces have been carefully cleaned and smeared with shellac or gold size, finally screwing evenly and firmly in position, locating the push rods.

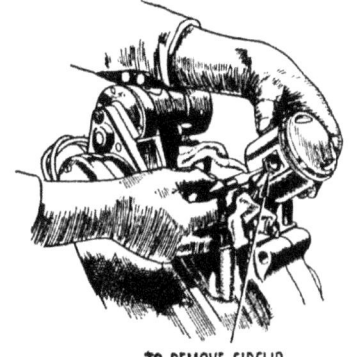

TO REMOVE CIRCLIP

FIG. 74. SHOWING HOW TO REMOVE CIRCLIP

In some instances it may be necessary to dismantle this unit. This can be done in the following way: Separate the halves of the case by releasing the screws. The rocker bushes are in two pieces, a tight fit in the body, with the ends flush. When assembling, the spindles, with the rockers, should be placed in the lower half case, after the joint faces have been cleaned of their oil joint compound and smeared with shellac or gold size, and the top half of the case should then be fitted. The cork washers should be placed on the spindles outside the case, and the support plates fitted, ensuring lateral pressure by tightening the spindle nuts.

The procedure is somewhat similar on other models, but it is rather more easy, since there is no oil circulation.

End play on the rockers can be corrected by withdrawing the bushes sufficiently to counter travel.

The Exhaust Lifter. The exhaust lifter abuts on the upper surface of the exhaust rocker in the case of Models L2/1 and 3/2. If, for any reason, the lever is detached from the shaft, refit it so that, when the abutment is resting on the rocker with the valve closed, it is in an approximately vertical position to be held just clear of contact by the spring on the cable adjuster.

On most other models the exhaust lifter works through the leverage of the rocker, abutting underneath an extension at the push rod end(s). This should be assembled so that, with the valve closed, the lifter has clearance of the rocker, the cable adjuster screwed right in, and the lever is as far rearwards as it will go. Then it should be secured on the squared shaft. This gives maximum adjustment on the cable.

The 1937-9 S.V. Engines. Very little dismantling is needed in order to decarbonize. First remove the plug and H.T. lead. Then unscrew the cylinder head bolts and lift the head off, followed by

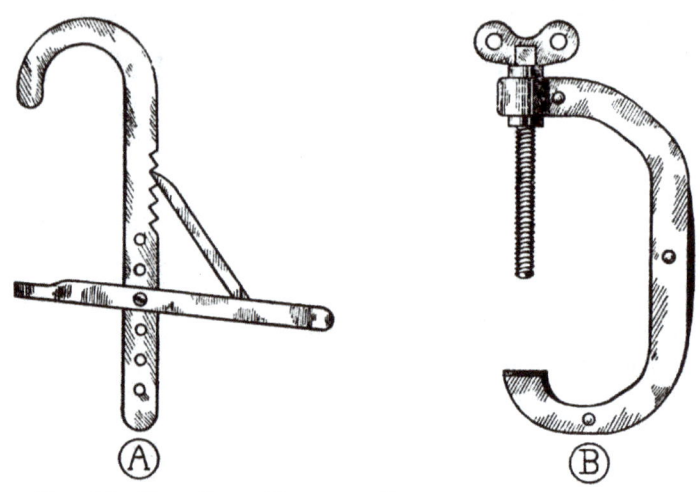

FIG. 75. TWO GOOD TYPES OF VALVE SPRING COMPRESSOR
The compressor shown at (A) is suitable for S.V. engines, while that illustrated at (B) is designed for O.H.V. engines. Both tools are of Terry manufacture

the cylinder head gasket. If it is intended to grind-in the valves, remove the cylinder barrel and take out the valves. To do this, compress each valve spring with a suitable valve spring compressor (obtainable from any accessory dealer).

A useful tool for valve extraction is shown at (A), Fig. 75. As soon as each valve spring is compressed the split collet can be removed and the valve spring, spring caps and valve withdrawn. Deal with the inlet and exhaust valves similarly and be careful not to interchange the valves; the exhaust valve generally is somewhat more discoloured than the inlet valve. To grind-in the valves, proceed as described on page 115.

Scrape off all carbon deposits from the piston crown with a blunt screwdriver and avoid scratching the aluminium alloy surface deeply. Also scrape off all carbon deposits from the combustion chamber and the cylinder head ports. As already mentioned, do not disturb the piston or rings unless absolutely necessary. Do not use emery cloth on the piston, but the combustion chamber may be polished if desired with emery-cloth if

OVERHAULING

all abrasive particles are afterwards cleaned out with a rag damped in petrol.

If the cylinder barrel has been drawn off the piston, a new gasket should be fitted between the barrel and crankcase when re-assembling. If the cylinder head gasket is in any way damaged or there are signs of "blowing," this gasket should also be replaced. Grease the cylinder head gasket liberally before replacing it, and tighten down the head bolts uniformly in a diagonal order. Work from the centre outwards, tightening the two bolts in the centre of the cylinder head first, then the centre one on the outside next to the sparking plug hole, next the one opposite to it, and finally those on the four corners. Now warm up the engine and again go over the cylinder and cylinder head nuts and bolts with a spanner to ensure that they are dead tight. Check and if necessary adjust the tappets (page 91), and everything is O.K. for a trial run. A new cylinder head gasket beds down to some extent, and therefore after covering a few hundred miles the cylinder head bolts should again be tightened down.

The 1937-9 Single-cylinder O.H.V. Engines. On these models it is necessary to raise the petrol tank before starting to decarbonize. The screw which secures the instrument panel should first be removed and the panel lifted until the nut securing the oil pipe to the gauge is accessible. Do not interfere with the electrical wiring. Now detach the oil pipe and then remove the petrol tank securing bolts. Raise the petrol tank, but before doing this cover up the front end with a duster to prevent scratching of the enamel. Also remove the saddle nose bolt and draw back the saddle cover by placing a piece of string over the front end of it and looping this back to the number plate. The purpose of doing this is to give the tank adequate clearance at the rear end.

Disconnect the H.T. lead and remove the sparking plug. Also disconnect the exhaust lifter cable, cylinder torque stay, carburettor and exhaust pipe. Remove the pair of banjo unions at the rocker spindles and take off the oil pipe which feeds the rocker box. Next remove the four cylinder head fixing bolts, undoing these evenly to prevent straining the head. On the 250 c.c., 350 c.c. engines it is necessary first to take off the two horizontal bolts on the off-side and remove the vertical plate. Now lift off the cylinder head complete with rocker box. Cover up the cylinder barrel with a cloth unless it is intended to remove the barrel in order to examine the piston and rings (see page 106). Removal of the piston itself is dealt with on page 104.

To remove the valves, take the rocker box off the cylinder head and then using a suitable valve spring compressor such as that shown at (B), Fig. 75, compress each valve spring until the split collet can be removed from the groove in the valve stem, and the spring, spring caps, and valve withdrawn. Remove both valves similarly and avoid mixing them up as they are *not* interchangeable. It should be noted that there is a valve spring seating washer under the exhaust valve spring, but not under the inlet

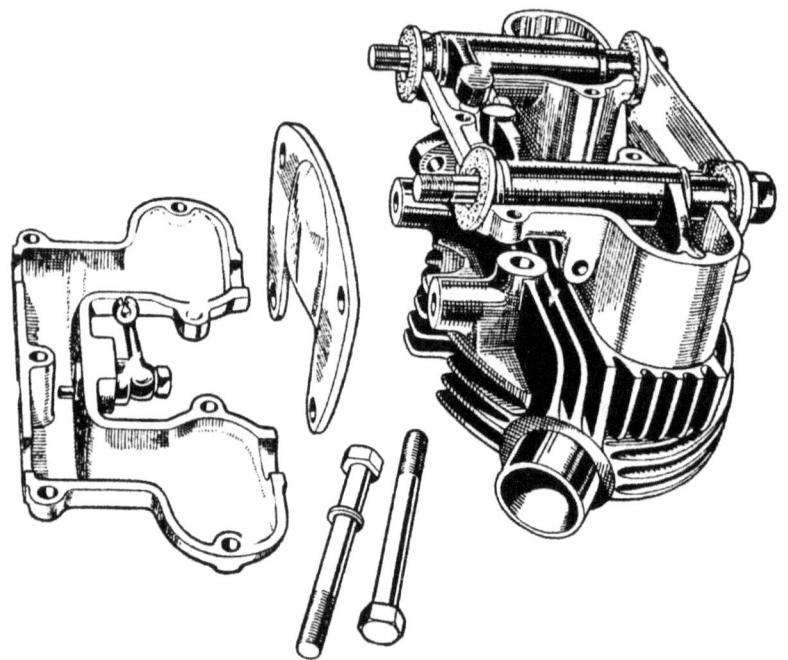

Fig. 76. Details of 1937–9 Cylinder Head and Rocker Box
This is applicable to all 250, 350 c.c. O.H.V. engines

valve spring. Remove all carbon deposits as previously described for the S.V. engines (page 106).

It is worth while inspecting the push rods and also the washers at the top and bottom of the push rod cover tubes. If the push rod ends are badly worn, new rods should be fitted. It is desirable to renew the washers whether these appear worn or not. Valve grinding is dealt with on page 115.

No cylinder head gasket is provided on the single-cylinder O.H.V. engines, and before replacing the head on the cylinder barrel it should be ground on to the head with some *fine* grade grinding paste (such as Richford's). Afterwards all traces of grinding paste must be most carefully removed. Smear a little engine oil on to the upper face of the cylinder barrel before refitting the head and see that both joint faces are absolutely clean. Refit the rocker box on the cylinder head and replace the

OVERHAULING

two together. New rocker box gaskets should be used and special care should be taken to tighten down the rocker box fixing bolts evenly and gradually. When replacing the cylinder head and rocker box, see that the push rods are properly located and that the cylinder head bolts are firmly and uniformly retightened.

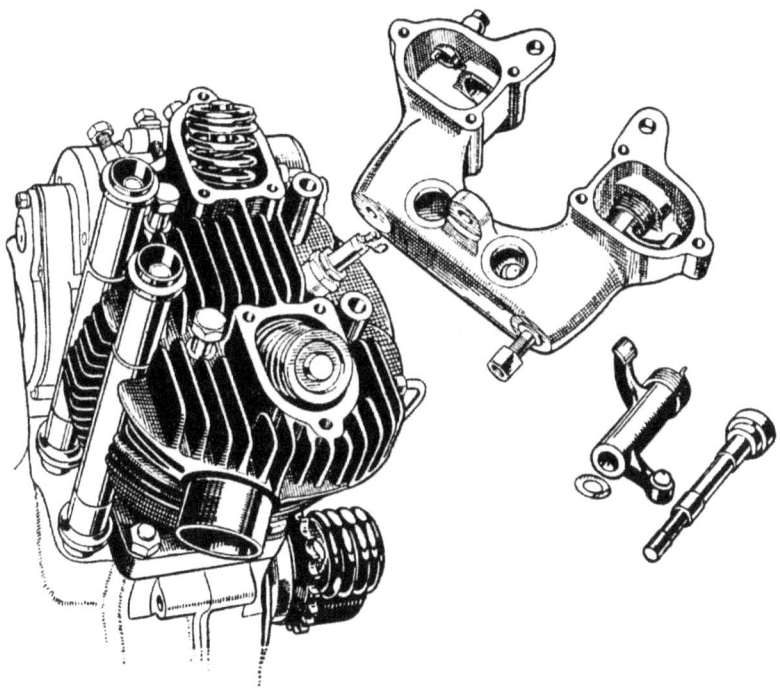

FIG. 77. DETAILS OF 1937-9 CYLINDER HEAD AND ROCKER BOX
Above is shown the arrangement on the 500 c.c. single-cylinder models

Before fitting the banjo unions to the rocker spindles the copper washers should be annealed by heating them over a gas ring so as to soften them and guarantee an oil-tight joint. Warm up the engine and again check the bolts for tightness. Adjust the tappets and the engine is ready for service.

WARNING—DON'T WARM UP IN CLOSED GARAGE

To Dismantle Rocker Box (1937-9 O.H.V. Singles). To remove the overhead rockers from the rocker box, tap out the spindles from the threaded ends, using a copper or hide mallet or else a hammer and piece of hardwood. If an ordinary hammer is used, the threads will probably be damaged. Re-assembly is straightforward, but see that the end thrust washers and rocker return springs are correctly replaced. Re-assemble in the following manner: replace the rocker and insert the spring with its end in the hole provided in the rocker arm. Insert the spindle and push

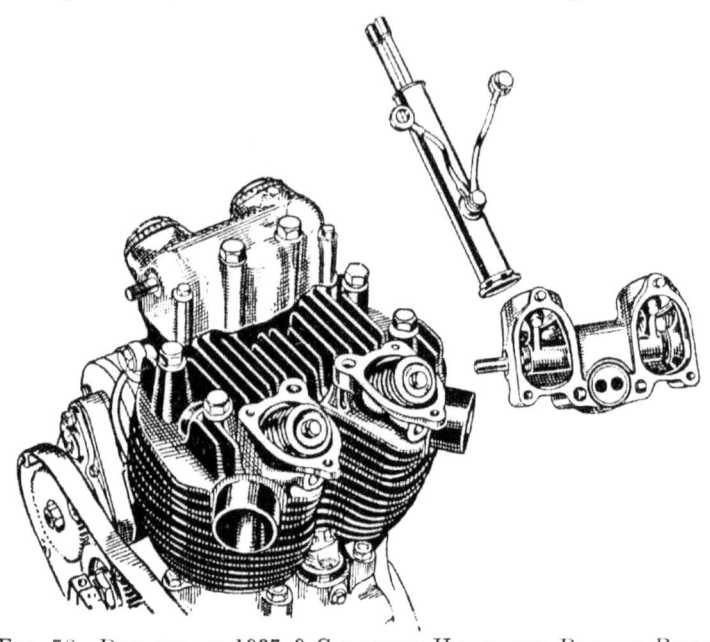

FIG. 78. DETAILS OF 1937-9 CYLINDER HEAD AND ROCKER BOXES
This applies to the Triumph twin-cylinder engines

it in far enough to enable it to mate up correctly with the outer end of the spring. Next apply a screwdriver to the slotted end of the spindle and twist the spindle round so as to tension the spring; finally force home into the rocker box casting. The locating peg on the spindle must be correctly positioned in the slot formed in the rocker box.

To Dismantle 1938-9 Twin-cylinder Engines. Dismantling procedure in the case of the 1938, 1939 "Speed Twin" and "Tiger 100" engines is very similar to that employed when decarbonizing the single-cylinder O.H.V. engines, but the following should be noted. Just underneath the petrol tank there is a joint in the oil pipe to the gauge which makes it unnecessary to lift the instrument panel. Eight bolts secure the cylinder head. Four of these also pass through the rocker boxes. Turn the petrol tank over sideways a little to facilitate removal of the cylinder head bolts. Lift off the cylinder head complete with the rocker boxes from the cylinder block as in the case of single-cylinder O.H.V. engines. Be careful not to lose the copper washers when removing the oil return pipes which connect to the cylinder head and push rod cover tubes. When re-assembling the rocker boxes, fit new gaskets and see that the tappets and push rods are correctly located when replacing the cylinder head. Tighten down the cylinder head evenly, working from the centre outwards. A copper plate is fitted between the cylinder block and head and this does not require renewing except after big mileages. However, it is beneficial to anneal the plate by heating over a gas ring. After re-assembly is complete, adjust the tappets (page 91), warm up the engine, and again check the nuts and bolts for tightness.

3T De Luxe. It is necessary to deal with dismantling and re-assembling the 1946-9 Triumphs in detail, as these machines vary considerably from earlier models. To dismantle the 350 c.c. models the following procedure should be adopted—
1. Disconnect H.T. cables and remove the plugs, then disconnect the exhaust pipes, carburettor and engine steady bracket.
2. Remove the two banjo unions at the rocker spindles and take off the rocker gear feed pipe. 3. Remove the cylinder head by unscrewing the four centre bolts and the four bolts sunk in the head fins; raise the cylinder head, detach the push rods and push rod tubes, and then lift the head off the cylinder block. 4. A valve spring compressor is necessary for the removal of the valves. Compress the valve springs and detach the valve spring cotters by means of a screwdriver. Mark the valve to facilitate replacement. 5. The rocker gear should not be stripped, provided the rocker arms are free on their spindles. To remove, tap the spindles out from the threaded end (using a soft tool) and extract the rocker arm from the rocker box. 6. If the cylinder block is to be removed it can be raised clear of the crankcase studs, but before doing this place a short $\frac{1}{4}$ in. bolt between the tappet grooves to prevent the tappets falling into the crankcase. 7. To take off the pistons, remove the two circlips and tap out the gudgeon pins clear of the connecting rod, using a soft drift. When doing this it is necessary to support the opposite side of the piston. Mark the pistons to ensure proper re-assembly.

When about to re-assemble the engine, all parts should be laid out in their correct order—this applies to all Triumph models. To re-assemble the 350 c.c. 3T de Luxe proceed as follows—
1. See the gaps in the piston rings are not in line, replace, and make sure the circlips are positioned correctly. 2. Before returning the cylinder block, grease the base washer and fit to block; fit the tappets and secure against falling into the crankcase with

rubber bands. Fit the block to the crankcase; on the base flange there is a "DS" mark and this must be on the drive side of the engine. 3. Fit rubber washers to the push rod tubes; grease the upper push rod tube washers and the cylinder head gasket, and fit the cylinder head. 4. The inlet push rods and tubes can now be fitted to the head; this is rendered more easy, as the lower push rod tube cups are marked with a vertical line which should be centralized and placed facing the magneto and dynamo respectively. The four centre holding-down bolts and the torque bracket should then be fitted to the cylinder head and placed in position on the cylinder block. 5. Raise the cylinder head about 1 in. when fitting the exhaust push rods; raise by means of a piece of wood on each side between the cylinder head fin and the block fin. The inlet and exhaust push rods should be positioned on the tappets, then the pieces of wood may be removed and the cylinder head lowered gently on to the block. See that the rocker balls are correctly assembled to the push rod cups. Finally, lightly tighten the four centre bolts. 6. The four remaining bolts should be fitted and the cylinder head tightened down evenly. 7. Tappet adjustment and replacement of covers follow next. 8. Refit torque to frame clip, carburettor, plugs, H.T. cables, rocker oil feed pipe and exhaust pipes. 9. Start the engine and carry out stationary tests. Stop the engine and re-tighten all nuts and bolts.

Tiger " 100 " and Speed Twin. Dismantling is carried out in the following order: 1. The screw securing the instrument panel should be removed, and the panel lifted until the union nut on the oil gauge pipe is accessible; detach the oil pipe (to prevent damage when the tank is lifted); remove the four tank bolts and the petrol pipe; take out the saddle nose bolt, and tie back the saddle to the back of the number plate by means of a loop of string; then raise the tank to the required height, but before doing this place a duster over the front end of the tank to prevent scratching the handlebar brackets. 2. Disconnect the H.T. cables and remove the plugs. 3. Disconnect the torque stays, carburettor and exhaust pipes. 4. Remove the two banjo unions at the rocker spindles and take off the rocker gear feed pipe. 5. Unscrew the four central cylinder head holding-down bolts, the four rocker box screws and the four stud nuts, and remove the rocker boxes. 6. To remove the rockers from the rocker box, the spindles should be tapped out with a soft tool from the threaded end; observe the positions of the rocker spindle thrust washers before performing this operation. 7. Next the front push rod tube and push rods should be removed, then the four remaining cylinder head bolts can be unscrewed and the cylinder head lifted off the block; remove the inlet push rod tube and push rods. 8. A valve spring compressor is required for removing the valves. Should such a tool not be available, a piece of wood can be cut to fit the shape of the cylinder head combustion chamber; this will prevent the valve dropping when pressure is exerted on the spring collar. Another piece of wood (hard wood should be chosen) should be suitably slotted for pressing down on the valve spring collar so that the cotters are exposed, then they can be tapped out with a screwdriver. Mark the valves to aid replacement. 9. Great care must be taken when removing the cylinder block that the tappets do not drop into the crankcase; place a rubber band round the heads of the tappets prior to lifting. If there is a possibility of the piston rings being broken, the pieces must be prevented from falling into the crankcase; do this by raising the pistons to their highest position, lifting the block a little and placing a clean cloth or two pieces of cardboard over the crankcase aperture. 10. Take off the pistons by removing the two circlips and tapping the gudgeon pins with a soft drift, care being taken to support the opposite side of the piston meanwhile. Mark the pistons for correct re-positioning.

To re-assemble the Tiger "100" and Speed Twin: 1. See the gaps in the piston rings are not in line; replace the pistons, and make certain the circlips are positioned correctly. 2. Place clips over the piston to secure the rings. 3. Grease the base washer and fit to block; fit the tappets and clip together with a rubber band; replace block over the pistons. 4. Remove piston ring clips, and assemble block to crankcase; grease and fit cylinder head gasket to block. 5. The push rod rubber washers can now be fitted over the tappet blocks, then the inlet push rods and tubes should be positioned to the tappet block. 6. Replace the cylinder head complete with manifold on the cylinder block, and tighten the four outside bolts lightly. 7. Fit inlet rocker box to cylinder head; check positioning of push rods to rocker balls; the same procedure is adopted with the exhaust rocker box and push rods. 8. Fit the four centre cylinder head bolts, and tighten down evenly. 9. Adjust the valve tappets (0·001 clearance). 10. Replace plugs, H.T. cables, torque stays, carburettor, rocker oil feed pipe and exhaust pipes. 11. Replace petrol tank and saddle, connect up oil pressure gauge and tighten down instrument panel. 12. Start the engine and carry out stationary tests. Stop the engine and re-tighten all nuts and bolts.

Decarbonizing (1935-6 Models). This the average motor-cyclist can do quite satisfactorily. It is necessary when there is an increasing tendency to pink and overheat, when the running is sluggish and there is a general loss of " tune." but in the majority of cases decarbonizing is only necessary after several thousand miles have been covered.

The following hints may prove useful: Cover all openings, such as cylinder barrel, and crankcase orifice, with a cloth, so that all foreign matter is prevented from entering; treat the overhead rocker gear as a whole, unless it is necessary to dismantle for some other purpose, this applying particularly to Models L2/1, 2/1, and 3/2, which are of the totally enclosed type. And the position of all washers, etc., should be carefully remembered, so as to ensure that they are returned to their correct positions, and the piston or pistons should always be restored to the original position.

Decarbonizing (1937-9 Models). When a decline in power output, loss of compression, and a tendency to knocking under slight provocation occur, it is an indication that decarbonizing is needed. In the case of side-valve engines it is usually necessary to decarbonize about every 2000 miles, but with overhead-valve engines it is generally sufficient to decarbonize after the first 2000 miles and then at intervals of 3000 to 4000 miles. Raising of the petrol tank is a necessary preliminary to decarbonizing the O.H.V. models, but not the S.V. machines with detachable cylinder heads. It is advisable to have a new gasket (where fitted) at hand before starting on the job of decarbonizing.

The Triumph Engineering Co. do not advise the removal of the cylinder barrel each time the engine is decarbonized and the barrel should be withdrawn only when it is desired to inspect the piston rings or to remove the piston. It will be found best to disturb the piston rings as seldom as possible so long as the engine performance remains good.

Valve Treatment (1935-6). Scrape the valve surfaces lightly and clean with a petrol-soaked cloth. The valve must seat evenly, showing a uniformly bright ring all round its circumference; if the valve is faulty in this respect it should be ground-in (see page 115).

Before refitting the valve, see that the condition of the collets and recess is such that perfect security is secured and that the springs have full tension. In the case of Model 6/1 it is important to see that the valves are returned to the cylinders from which they were removed. A specially designed tool to aid valve removal can be obtained from the Triumph Service Department.

If the valve guides are worn they should be replaced, since air leaks reduce the efficiency of the engine. These guides are a driving fit in the cylinder casting; they can be knocked out by means of a punch of soft metal, and new bushes can be fitted in the same way. If possible, have the valve seat recut with a proper tool in alignment with the guide when new ones are fitted.

Decarbonizing (1946-9). The 1946-9 Triumph should run for 8000 or 10,000 miles before it requires decarbonizing; this work should be done only when there is a falling off in power, loss of compression, noisy operation, or more difficult starting. The cylinder block need not be removed when decarbonizing; in fact, the factory strongly recommend that this part should not be taken off unless new piston rings are to be fitted, or other work done to the engine which necessitates removal of the barrel.

So as to remove all carbon from inaccessible places, it is a wise plan, if convenient, to boil the cylinder head in a solution of caustic soda, but in the case of the 500 c.c. models the induction manifold should not be left attached to the cylinder head as caustic soda adversely affects aluminium. There is, however, one snag to boiling in soda; it takes the paint off the cylinder head, but if this be liberally black-leaded before re-assembly its appearance is not impaired. When decarbonizing in the ordinary way, avoid scratch marks, particularly on the valve seatings.

The top of the pistons and the cylinder block (in position) should be washed in petrol before removal of the carbon deposit. Loose carbon must be kept away from the edge of the pistons, as far as possible; afterwards any particles which remain can be blown out by means of the tyre pump. A useful tool for removing the carbon from the piston crown is a stick of solder hammered out flat at the end, as this does not scratch. New circlips should be obtained if the pistons are removed, as the old ones may have lost their tension. Remove the carbon from the upper rim of the cylinder bore, and clean the cylinder block fins by means of a wire brush.

The valve springs should be examined carefully for cracks and fatigue; a set of new springs should be fitted if necessary.

Grinding-in the Valves. When decarbonizing it is worth while removing the valves and carefully inspecting them. If the valve faces show signs of slight pitting the valves should be ground-in, but if the pitting is extensive, the proper course is to have the valves refaced at a garage or by the makers. Excessive grinding-in should never be undertaken because this causes the valve seats to deepen and the valves to become "pocketed." Generally it is not necessary to grind-in the valves more frequently than once every alternate decarbonizing. On side-valve engines it is necessary to press the valves down on their seats while grinding-in, using a screwdriver in the slots provided on the valve heads. In the case of overhead-valve engines, however, the valves have to be pulled up against their seats with the aid of a small valve grinding tool (obtainable from accessory dealers). When grinding-in smear a little fine grinding paste (such as Richford's) on the valve face and insert the valve in its guide. Then, using a steady pressure on the valve grinding tool, rotate the valve on its seat about a third of a turn in one direction and then the same amount in the other. Every half-dozen or so oscillations lift the valve off its seat and turn it round slightly. This prevents the formation of "rings." Continue grinding-in until the valve face and its seat come up bright for a considerable depth. Perfect line contact is not good enough. Stop grinding-in when no "cut" is felt, and remove the valve to put some more grinding paste on it. Be very careful not to get any of the paste anywhere except on the valve faces, and after grinding-in remove every trace of the abrasive, and wash the valves in petrol. Any carbon deposits should be removed before starting to grind-in. If the split collet grooves are ragged or worn, replace the valves or serious damage may ensue. Test the valves for play in their guides. A worn inlet valve guide causes poor starting and slow running. When re-assembling the valves it is advantageous to smear the stems with a little Colloidal Graphite upper cylinder lubricant.

Valve grinding in the case of the 1946-9 models should be carried out if, after examination, the valve faces are seen to be pitted. If this be so, they should be re-faced at a garage, as the grinding necessary, if done in the home garage, also grinds away the seating, which is undesirable. The valve stems should be examined, carefully cleaned and polished before the grinding is started. The valve head and the exposed portion of the valve stem should be cleaned of carbon deposit. Inspect the groove which retains the split cotters; if worn, renew, because if the cotters are not securely located extensive damage to the engine may result. Grinding compound is used. A little should be smeared on the face of the valve; the valve placed in position, and rotated backwards and forwards on the seating, lifted and given half a turn after every twenty seconds so as to prevent a particle of the compound cutting a groove in any one place. Remove the valve, wash in petrol and examine to note how the grinding operation is proceeding after a short time. A finely ground surface round the face of the valve is the object in view, so the grinding should be continued until both valve face and seating assume an even grey bearing without any marks. When it is considered that the process is completed, clean off both face and seating with petrol, dry, and make pencil marks on the valve, across the grinding marks, round the whole surface of the face. Replace the valve dry, and revolve it a few times. All the pencil marks will have disappeared if the operation is completed; if not, continue grinding

OVERHAULING

until a further test proves a perfect seating has been secured. Lubricate the stem of the valve with a colloidal graphite upper cylinder lubricant before re-assembling the valve. For a few pence you can buy a small quantity, if you take your own bottle.

The push rod tubes should be examined for dents and slackness of the caps; the push rods checked for wear by fitting the push rod ends to the ball end of the valve rocker, for if wear has taken place the push rod end will foul the rocker arm when the latter is at its working angle.

All rubber, composition and paper washers should be renewed when re-assembling; copper cylinder head gaskets can be annealed, and need only be renewed about every three or four decarbonizations.

The Clutch (1935-6). The correct way of gaining access is explained under Adjustments, Chapter VII.

The correct order for dismantling is: If the chain wheel is dismantled, remove the primary chain by taking out the split link. The arrangement of the plates as they are taken down should be carefully noted, for they must be restored in the same order, and on no account must metal-to-metal contact be allowed. If the centre or driven member is dislodged, remember to replace the nut locking washer. In the case of cork clutch, any sign of burning or uneven wear implies the renewal of the inserts—this replugging is an operation standardized by the Triumph Service Department at a small charge.

The order of assembly with cork clutches, excepting in the case of Model 6/1, is: centre secured to the shaft by locknut and washer; chain wheel, after greasing the bearing; driven or dished plate, convex side outwards; driven plate; driving plate; driven plate; driving plate; and outer pressure plate, with spring, nuts, etc., properly assembled, as explained under Adjustments, Chapter VII.

With Model 6/1, the chain wheel is not plugged and it is followed by a dished plate having a large centre and eight surrounding smaller holes. Continue with the driven, plugged plate and follow with the remainder, as above.

With Ferodo-lined clutches—L2/1 and 3/1—the order is: driven member, fixed as before; chain wheel with ferodo disk in the rear recess and with bearings greased; ferodo disk; dished plate, convex side outwards; ferodo disk; driving plate, the turned end of the dogs outwards; ferodo ring; pressure plate; and springs, as before.

The Clutch (1946-9). The outer portion of the primary chain case must be removed to obtain access to the clutch. First take off the footrest and the brake pedal, the latter after removing the securing nut. The removal of the chain cover screws necessitates the use of a large screwdriver. Lie the machine on the offside footrest, as this allows more pressure to be applied on the screwdriver. Give the outer half of the cover a tap with a mallet or hammer handle to separate the two halves; on no account use a screwdriver or other tool, as damage to the faces may result. Note the tubular distance piece fitted to the footrest rod between the case and the frame; this must be replaced when re-assembling.

Using the special key provided, remove the four brass clutch nuts to dismantle the plates. On the underside of the head of each nut there is a small "pip" to prevent the nut from unscrewing; insert a knife blade under the head of each nut when turning it to prevent the "pip" engaging with the end of the clutch spring. The outer pressure plate and the driven and driving plates can be removed when the nuts have been taken off their pins. In the 350 c.c. models there are three cork and four steel plates; in the 500 c.c. machines there are four cork and five steel plates.

Examine the plates. The corks should project $\frac{1}{32}$ in. on each side of the plate, they should be in an oily state, and the steel plates should be smooth and not scored, while the tongues of the cork plates should be unworn. Compare the length of the clutch springs with a new one; if not the same, fit new ones. The clutch hub can be removed from the gear-box mainshaft after taking off the nuts and washers by means of the withdrawal tool provided. When the clutch is withdrawn, the clutch housing and sprocket revolve on the clutch hub on a bearing consisting of twenty $\frac{1}{4}$ in. by $\frac{1}{4}$ in. rollers; examine the bearing surfaces for wear.

When re-assembling, re-fitting the clutch hub to the mainshaft is a simple task, but care should be taken that the key is positioned and the nut fully tightened on the washer. Before installing on the mainshaft, the housing and sprocket should be fitted to the hub. Grease the roller bearing. Note that the clutch studs are fitted into their slots before re-assembling the plates. Soak the corked plates in oil or a mixture of engine oil and paraffin, half and half, before they are assembled. Fit a plain plate first, then a corked one, and so on with a plain plate last on the outside of the clutch, and cover with the pressure plate. Replace the clutch springs in their cups, then screw the four nuts into the pins. The nuts should be screwed up until the ends of the pins are level with the heads of the screws when new corked plates are fitted; if the corks are a little worn, rather more pressure may be necessary on the springs.

When the clutch has been re-assembled a final adjustment is necessary. Extract the clutch by means of the handlebar lever and spin with the kick-starter while someone looks down on to it to see that it spins true. Adjustment of the clutch nuts is indicated if the pressure plate wobbles when the clutch is spun. The plate can be made to spin correctly by screwing the nut adjacent to the part of the pressure plate which is nearest to the edge of the housing, repeating the process until it runs true. It is essential to adjust this part correctly; otherwise the clutch will not free properly, causing difficult gear changing and trouble when selecting bottom gear from neutral.

To Dismantle 1938-9 Twist-grip. To dismantle the twist-grip throttle control (Fig. 79), peel back the rubber grip and withdraw

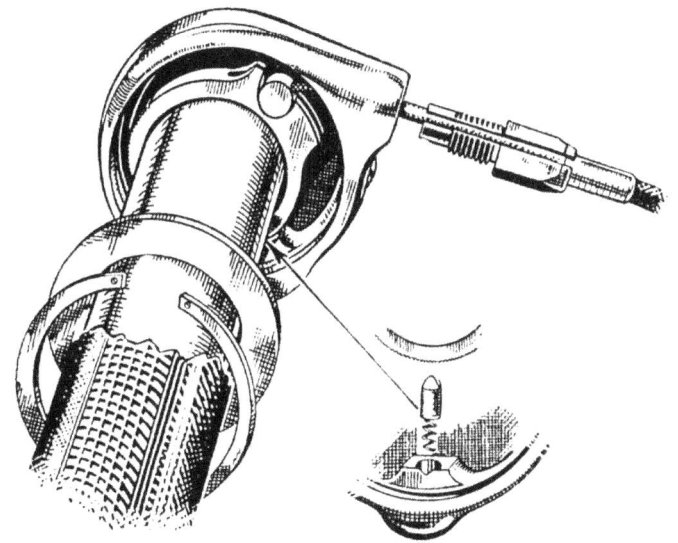

FIG. 79. 1938-9 TWIST-GRIP CONTROL

the spring ring and washer. Then unscrew the cable stop and draw out the cable. Now draw off the grip. When doing this, be careful not to lose the small plunger and spring which provided the excellent click action.

When re-assembling, the order is reversed, but it is necessary to revolve the grip when re-inserting the cable, so that the grip picks up the cable nipple and draws it into place.

A new type friction twist grip has been designed to enable the rider to adjust the tension as desired. Adjustment is by a knurled thumb adjuster screw. The new grip is now fitted to the 3T de Luxe, Speed Twin, and Tiger "100."

Re-enamelling. The general appearance of the motor-cycle is seldom improved if the frame only be touched up here and there with enamel. In the event of an accident happening it is advisable for the sake of preserving the metal, but as a general rule it is not to be advised. It is much better to wait until the time of the annual overhaul and then do the job properly.

The machine will at this time be completely dismantled; hence the work is rendered more easy. Before re-enamelling the whole cycle must be thoroughly cleaned, but this need not occupy much time. Every trace of dust, dirt and oil must be removed before the first coat of enamel is applied. If this be not done the final appearance of the machine will be ruined. The gear-box can best be cleaned with petrol and a clean rag; the enamel parts with paraffin, then a cloth soaked in petrol to remove the paraffin, and finally dried.

CHAPTER IX

1946 AND 1949 TRIUMPH MODELS

It is interesting to note that the Triumph Engineering Company was one of the first to be ready for the change-over from wartime to peace-time production, but more interesting still that, by planning well in advance, this well-known factory was actually in a position to introduce a new-model range for the 1946 season; a series of motor-cycles which embody up-to-date practice in numerous directions.

A departure which has gained the full approval of the motor-cycling public is the application of the vertical twin O.H.V. engine to the 350 c.c. class; an innovation on which the factory is to be congratulated. The 3T de Luxe is a touring machine of undoubted quality and performance, as it provides easy starting at all times, a high degree of riding comfort, an unobtrusiveness which captivates, yet it is capable of an intriguing burst of speed.

There are also four models in the 500 c.c. class—the "Trophy" Trials machine, the "Grand Prix" racing machine (details of these two new models, specially designed for sporting enthusiasts, will be found on pages 127 and 128), the Tiger "100" and the Speed Twin. The last-named was introduced in 1937, but the current edition incorporates many new features. It is designed for the motor-cyclist who desires smooth running, effortless riding, and a high all-round performance; the Tiger "100" is an ultra-fast mount for the enthusiastic rider.

All these models are definitely "new-season" mounts, although none is a radical departure from accepted Triumph practice; they are new models, because of the numerous specification changes which have been introduced. These may be referred to briefly.

The most outstanding is the adoption of the Triumph telescopic type of fork with hydraulically damped movement and automatic lubrication; a development promoting riding comfort, perfect steering, and road holding. The new fork has brought about a change in the operation of the front brake, the headlamp support, and in the general appearance of the machine. Another visible change, in the case of the 500 c.c. models, is the employment of a four-gallon capacity petrol tank.

A further important improvement is that the current for lighting is generated by a separate dynamo, while ignition is accounted for by a twin-cylinder B.T.H. magneto; the former gear-driven direct from the forward camshaft, and supported through the engine-plates behind the front down tube, and the latter in its normal position.

The appearance of the Triumph engine has always called forth favourable comment, but it has been improved by an alteration in the oil return system. This is now entirely internal, passage-ways being provided by drillings in the head and barrel, instead

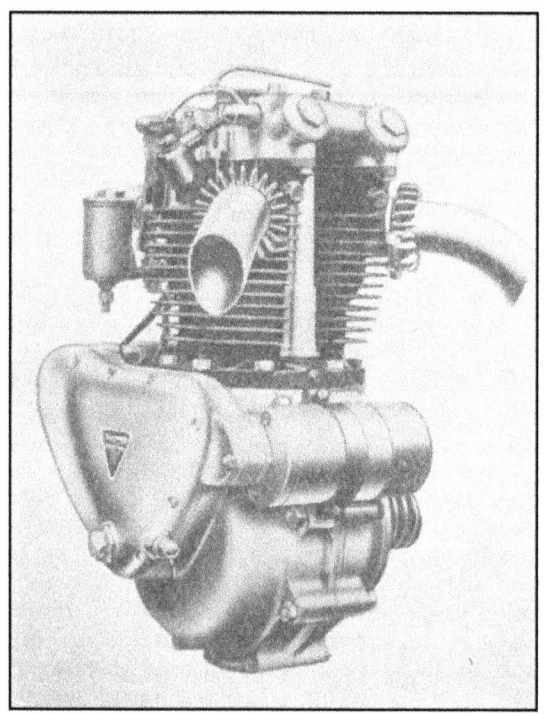

FIG. 80. VERTICAL TWIN ENGINE

of the external drain pipes leading from the rocker boxes to the push-rod enclosing tubes. The clean-cut appearance of the engine is seen in Fig. 80.

Among other notable changes are shifting the speedometer drive to the rear wheel; reducing the number of handlebar controls; the use of a spring loaded plunger for controlling the air, located close to the top of the carburettor; and automatic advance control of the magneto.

The 350 c.c. O.H.V. The specification of the 3T de Luxe 350 c.c. models is as follows—

Engine. New design vertical twin O.H.V. unit, double high

camshaft type; bore 55 mm., stroke 73·4 mm., capacity 349 c.c.; rocker box integral with cylinder head; patented crankshaft assembly with centrally disposed flywheel; high tensile alloy steel connecting rods; totally enclosed valve gear with duplex springs of areo quality; automatic advance magneto and easily accessible separate all-gear driven dynamo; pinions in special alloy gear steel; Amal carburettor with Triumph patented twist-grip control; full dry-sump lubrication with two plunger type pumps; positive feed to big ends and overhead valve gear; oil drained from rocker box without use of external piping.

FIG. 81. THE 3T DE LUXE

Transmission. Primary chain running in polished cast aluminium oil bath case; rear chain positively lubricated by feed from primary chain case, and protected on top and bottom runs; four-speed gear-box of Triumph patented design and manufacture; gears and shafts of hardened nickel-chrome steel; positive foot change, fully enclosed; large diameter multiplate clutch with accessible adjustment; gear ratios, 5·8, 6·95, 10·0 and 14·7 to 1.

Petrol Tank. All-steel welded of 3 gallon capacity; quick opening filler cap.

Oil Tank. All-steel welded with accessible filters, drain plug and separate vent; capacity ¾ gallon.

Frame. Full cradle type with large diameter front down tube.

Front Fork. New Triumph design and manufacture; telescopic type with large hydraulically damped movement and automatic lubrication; no adjustment necessary.

Brakes. Incorporating large braking area and finest quality brake lining material; front and rear brakes with finger adjustment.

Handlebar. Adjustable for height and reach; grouped adjustable control levers.

Mudguards. Wide "D" section guards with streamline stays; detachable tail piece to rear guard for easy wheel removal.

Wheels and Tyres. Improved design wheels, with special spoke lacing for maximum strength; 26 × 3·25 Dunlop tyres front and rear.

Toolbox. Large capacity all-steel construction, with weatherproof protection; complete set of good quality tools and grease gun.

FIG. 82. THE TIGER "100"

Equipment. Lucas 6-volt separate dynamo lighting, voltage controlled set; large diameter head lamp; electric horn; kneegrips; adjustable de Luxe saddle; downswept exhaust pipes.

The 500 c.c. O.H.V. "Twins." The specification of the Tiger "100" and the Speed Twin is as follows—

Engine. Double high camshaft O.H.V. vertical twin; bore 63 mm., stroke 80 mm., capacity 498 c.c.; compression ratio of 7·8 to 1 in the case of the Tiger "100" and 7 to 1 in the Speed Twin; low expansion alloy pistons; cylinder head and barrel in special cast iron; high tensile aluminium alloy crankcase of great strength and rigidity; patented crankshaft incorporating integral balance weights and centrally disposed flywheel; "H" section connecting rod in R.R. 56 Hiduminium alloy, with patented lined big ends; all moving parts polished (Tiger "100" only); automatic advance magneto and separate dynamo all-gear driven; totally enclosed and positively lubricated valve gear; duplex aero quality valve springs; dry-sump lubrication system incorporating accessible plunger type pumps with positive feed to big ends and valve gear; excess oil drained without external pipes.

Transmission. Primary chain running in oil bath case; rear chain positively lubricated by feed from primary chaincase, and protected on top and bottom runs; four-speed gear-box of Triumph patented design and manufacture; gears and shafts of hardened nickel-chrome steel; patented positive foot change, fully enclosed; large diameter multiplate clutch, with accessible adjustment; gear ratios (solo), 5·0, 6·0, 8·65 and 12·7 to 1.

FIG. 83. THE SPEED TWIN

Carburettor. Large bore Amal carburettor and induction pipe, with Triumph patented quick action twist-grip throttle control.

Petrol Tank. All-steel welded; quick opening filler cap; rubber mounted instrument panel; capacity 4 gallons.

Oil Tank. All-steel welded, with accessible filters, drain plug and separate vent; capacity 1 gallon.

Frame. Brazed full cradle type, constructed from tubes of finest alloy steel; large diameter tapered front down tube.

Front Fork. New Triumph development; telescopic with large movement, hydraulically damped; automatic lubrication; no adjustments necessary.

Brakes. Triumph design with large braking area and finest quality lining material; finger adjustment for front and rear.

Handlebar. Adjustable for height and reach; long type brake and clutch levers.

Mudguards. Of adequate width with streamline section stays; detachable tail piece to rear guard for easy wheel removal.

Wheels and Tyres. Triumph design wheels, spokes specially laced to take braking and transmission stresses; Dunlop tyres, front 26 × 3·25, rear 26 × 3·50.

Toolbox. All-steel construction of large capacity, with weatherproof protection; complete set of good quality tools and grease gun.

Equipment. Lucas 6-volt dynamo lighting set, with voltage control, large diameter chrome head lamp and electric horn; adjustable de Luxe saddle; downswept exhaust pipes.

The smart appearance of the well-planned 1946 Triumph motor-cycles is considerably enhanced by the excellence of their finish. This may be mentioned in some little detail.

The 3T de Luxe model petrol tank panels, mudguards and wheel rim centres are lined in ivory; plated parts in chromium; unplated parts in black enamel.

The Tiger "100" petrol tank is chromium plate, with silver sheen panels lined out in blue; the mudguards, silver sheen with black centre strip; the wheels, chromium plated rims and spokes, silver sheen rim centres lined in blue; frame black enamel.

The Speed Twin is particularly attractive in finish. The frame, forks, etc., are in amaranth dark red; petrol tank chromium plated with red panels and lined in gold; wheels in chromium plate with red hubs and rim centres (lined in gold); handlebar and exhaust pipe chromium plated; and all bolts and nuts cadmium plated.

The current 3T de Luxe, Speed Twin, and Tiger "100" models incorporate a number of improvements. These are discussed elsewhere, so they need not be repeated here.

" Trophy " Trials Machine. The "Trophy" model TR5 is a machine which has been designed throughout to compete successfully in the most exacting and arduous trial or scramble. It is light in weight (295 lb. dry and without lighting set), remarkably easy to handle, and the engine, though specially tuned for reliable slow running, has plenty of power for the highest speeds when necessary. It is altogether an interesting machine built to cater for the sporting rider, and meets his requirements in every possible way.

The following is the specification of this fascinating mount—

Engine. Vertical twin cylinder with gear driven double high camshafts; bore 63 mm., stroke 80 mm.—498 c.c.; bi-metal cylinder and head with cast-in liners and valve inserts; special cams; totally enclosed and positively lubricated valve gear; duralumin pushrods; high tensile aluminium alloy crankcase; "H" section connecting rods in R.R.56 Hiduminium alloy with patented plain big ends; patented crankshaft mounted on massive ball bearings with central flywheel; full dry sump

1946 AND 1949 TRIUMPH MODELS

lubrication by plunger type pumps with positive feed to big ends and valve gear; Amal carburettor with Triumph design Vokes air-cleaner; manually operated B.T.H. waterproof magneto.

Transmission. Primary chain in polished light-alloy oil bath case; rear chain adequately protected and lubricated; Triumph four-speed wide-ratio gear-box; hardened nickel-chrome steel

FIG. 84. "TROPHY" TRIALS MACHINE

gears and shafts; patented positive stop foot-change; large diameter multiplate clutch; folding kickstarter; gear ratios, 5·24, 7·60, 12·02, 16·08.

Petrol Tank. Narrow all-steel welded design, capacity 2½ gallons; quick release filler, twin racing type taps.

Oil Tank. All-steel welded, with accessible filters, drain plug and separate vent; capacity ¾ gallon.

Frame. Special competition frame, light in weight and with ample ground clearance; gives light and accurate steering at all speeds and over all types of going; 70 deg. steering lock.

Front Fork. Triumph telescopic pattern, hydraulically damped.

Brakes. Triumph design with finger adjustment front and rear.

Handlebar. Competition pattern, fully adjustable, chromium-plated levers.

Mudguards. Light alloy with tubular stays.

Wheels and Tyres. Triumph design wheels, 300 × 20 front, 400 × 19 rear. Dunlop Universal tyres.

Toolbox. All-steel large capacity with quick action fastener; complete set of good quality tools and grease gun.

Equipment. Lucas 6-volt dynamo lighting set with voltage control; quick release plug for easy removal of headlamp; saddle adjustable for height front and rear; upswept two-in-one exhaust pipe with tubular silencer; Smith's 120 m.p.h. chronometric speedometer; Lucas "Altette" horn.

Finish. Petrol tank chromium-plated with silver sheen panels

FIG. 85. "GRAND PRIX" RACING MACHINE

lined in blue; mudguards in silver sheen with black central strip; wheel rims chromium-plated with rim centres in silver sheen lined blue.

The unique Triumph spring wheel and the new prop stand are fitted as extras.

"Grand Prix" Racing Machine. The "Grand Prix" racing machine has been designed to enable owner-racing drivers to compete on level terms in International road racing. This machine is "owner-riders" only, because it is not Triumph policy to support racing with works' machines and works' teams. In the view of the Triumph Engineering Company a racing model should be part of the normal range, and so available for purchase by the public.

The final preparation of this model, before it is delivered to the purchaser, is such that the machine may be immediately taken to the road racing circuit, there to be raced with no further lightening, polishing or tuning. Its weight, with empty tanks, is 314 lb. It should be remembered that it is not intended to be ridden on public roads.

The engine is entirely new. The bore and stroke of this racing

1946 AND 1949 TRIUMPH MODELS

model are the same as those of the Tiger "100", but no part of the new engine is incorporated in any of the other power units of the Triumph range.

The specification and technical details are appended—

Engine. O.H.V. all-alloy vertical twin cylinder with two gear driven racing lift curve camshafts; bore 63 mm., stroke 80 mm.—498 c.c.; bi-metal cylinder and head with cast-in liners and valve inserts; cylinder head, ports and all moving parts, mirror polished; high duty alloy pistons; special forged connecting rods in R.R.56 Hiduminium alloy with plain bearing big ends; forged extra stiff built-up crankshaft in case-hardened nickel-chrome steel, mounted on heavy duty roller bearings with central flywheel; dry sump lubrication with large capacity plunger type pumps with positive feeds to big ends and valve gear; twin Amal carburettors with flexible feed pipes and remote float chamber; B.T.H. TT type gear driven magneto with handlebar control; exhaust pipes fitted with appropriate megaphones; each engine is individually assembled and brake tested before delivery.

Transmission. $\frac{1}{2}$ in. $\times$ 0·305 in. primary chain with guard and lubricator; $\frac{5}{8}$ in. $\times$ $\frac{3}{8}$ in. rear chain; Triumph four-speed gearbox fitted with special nickel-chrome shafts and gears and special dogging for easy gear changing; enclosed positive stop foot change; lightweight multiplate clutch with Ferodo inserts; gear ratios (see below).

Petrol Tank. All-steel welded; capacity $4\frac{1}{4}$ gallons, with quick action cap and separate vent.

Oil Tank. One gallon capacity with accessible filters, drain plug, separate vent and quick action cap.

Oil Filter. "Vokes" full-flow type in scavenge oil line.

Frame. Full cradle type, carefully brazed, finest quality alloy steel tubes and forged lugs.

Forks. Triumph telescopic pattern with hydraulic damping and steering damper lock.

Brakes. Special racing design, 8 in. $\times$ $1\frac{3}{8}$ in. front and rear; finger adjustment.

Handlebar. Racing pattern of alloy steel.

Mudguards. Narrow section in light alloy; conform with F.I.C.M. regulations; tubular stays.

Wheels and Tyres. Dunlop light alloy racing type rims; Dunlop racing tyres 300 $\times$ 20 ribbed front, 350 $\times$ 19 triple-studded rear.

Equipment. Smith's 80 $\times$ 100 revolution counter, rubber mounted; Terry saddle; sponge rubber mudguard pad.

Finish. Petrol tank chromium-plated with silver sheen panels lined blue; mudguards in silver sheen with black centre strip.

Rear Springing. Triumph spring wheel fitted as standard.

THE BOOK OF THE TRIUMPH

Gear Ratios

Engine Sprocket	Top	3rd	2nd	1st
22T	5·00	5·48	7·20	8·67
23T (Std)	4·78	5·24	6·88	8·26
24T	4·57	5·01	6·58	7·93

Pistons. Pistons can be supplied suitable for Pool petrol, Petrol-Benzol or Alcohol fuels. To be specified when ordering.

Carburettors. Main jets, according to requirements; valves, 6/4; needle jets, 0·109 (alcohol, 0·113).

Ignition. Nominal advance $\frac{7}{16}$ in.

Recommended Plugs. K.L.G. 689, Lodge R51, Champion LA15.

Recommended Oils. Any recognized first grade mineral oil.

Measurements. Saddle height, 29½ in.; wheelbase (static), 55 in.; overall length, 84 in.; overall width, 28 in.; ground clearance, 6 in.

Weight. Dry, 314 lb.

Performance. A machine to the quoted specification, on a dry tarmac road and running on Pool petrol, has attained speeds in excess of 120 m.p.h. (7,416 r.p.m.). The r.p.m. indicator is driven off the pinion that, in a standard model, would drive the dynamo; the drive passes through holes in the front engine plates.

CHAPTER X

FAULTS AND THEIR DIAGNOSIS

EVERY motor-cycle is liable to develop faults. If the machine is neglected, trouble is increased to a maximum; if it is cared for properly, trouble is reduced to a minimum. The pukka rider carries out routine maintenance jobs in the garage; he is seldom, if ever, called upon to make adjustments on the road, and he enjoys that peace of mind engendered by the knowledge that his mount is in perfect trim and that he will reach his destination without any enforced stoppage. The indifferent motor-cyclist leaves well alone until trouble is encountered; he experiences the vexation of having to tackle jobs of a more or less serious nature at the roadside—hardly the ideal place at the best of times, and particularly annoying if the weather is bad. Motor-cycles do, however, sometimes develop unexpected faults, despite the most careful servicing; hence the following hints on the easiest method of ascertaining what is wrong.

If any untoward defect manifests itself, the sooner it is discovered and remedied the better the rider is pleased. The arrangement of the information contained in this chapter is designed to enable the motor-cyclist to locate the trouble with the minimum expenditure of time and energy.

The figure before each possible cause in the various systems suggests the order in which the several components should be checked. Generally speaking, the most frequent cause of trouble is a defect or maladjustment of the carburation system; the second most likely cause is a fault in the ignition system. This is the *raison d'être* for the procedure recommended.

Engine Fails to Start

Carburation Failure.
1. Controls out of order.
2. Petrol supply exhausted.
3. Petrol tap fully or partially closed.
4. Petrol pipe obstructed.
5. Jet choked.
15. Air leakage.

Ignition Failure.
6. Weak spark.
7. Short circuit on plug terminal or lead.

8. Faulty plug.
9. Plug points sooted.
10. Plug points incorrectly adjusted.
11. Contact breaker arm sticking.
12. Contact breaker points dirty.
13. Contact breaker points incorrectly adjusted.
14. Contact breaker points not lined up correctly.
16. Failure in magneto insulation.

Should the engine fail to start, first of all check up the carburettor and petrol supply by seeing the controls are in order, there is fuel in the tank, the tap is fully open, there is no obstruction in the petrol pipe, and that the jet is not choked.

If the carburettor floods when the float needle is depressed, test for a spark at the plug points; if a spark shows, the fault may be a too-weak spark to fire under compression, or a short circuit on the plug terminal or lead. Should there be no spark at the plug, test for spark at the terminal; if there is such a spark, it indicates that the plug is faulty, the plug points dirty, the spark is weak (necessitating re-adjustment of the points), or a short circuit in the plug itself. No spark at the terminal suggests checking the contact breaker, since the trouble may be a sticking contact breaker arm, dirty points, incorrect gap between the points or badly aligned points. If the fault does not lie with any of the above, test for air leakage. In the unlikely event of the magneto insulation failing, this defect can only be detected by means of special tests.

Engine Runs Irregularly
Lack of Power

Carburation Failure.
1. Petrol pipe obstructed.
2. Jet choked.
3. Petrol filler cap vent obstructed.
5. Controls out of order.
13. Weak mixture.
14. Air leakage.

Conditional Failure.
4. Sticking valve.
6. Poor compression.
7. Incorrect valve clearances.
8. Valve needs grinding-in.

FAULTS AND THEIR DIAGNOSIS

9. Weak valve springs.
10. Choked silencer.
11. Valves incorrectly timed.
12. Excessive carbon deposit.

If the lack of power is only occasional the probable cause is a partial obstruction in the petrol pipe, a partially choked jet, an obstruction in the petrol filler cap vent, or a sticking valve. If the engine lacks power continuously, the cause may be one of the following: Controls out of order, poor compression, incorrect valve clearances, pitted valves, valve springs weak, silencer choked, obstruction in the flow of petrol, excessive carbon deposit, or a weak mixture due to the needle in the carburettor being set too low or an air leak at the carburettor joint.

Engine Fails on Hills

Ignition Failure.
3. Plug points sooted.
4. Ignition too far advanced.

Conditional Failure.
1. Excessive carbon deposit.
2. Valve clearances incorrect.

Engine Miss Fires

Carburation Failure.
5. Incorrect mixture strength.
6. Water in petrol.
7. Petrol pipe obstructed.
8. Choked jet.

Ignition Failure.
1. Contact breaker arm sticking.
2. Plug points sooted.
3. Contact breaker points dirty.
4. Occasional short circuit.

The engine misses fire if the contact breaker arm is sticking, plugs sooted, contact breaker points dirty or if there is an occasional short circuit in the ignition system. If this system is not at fault, the cause is an incorrect mixture, water in the petrol (very unlikely, unless the weather be very stormy), or a starved carburettor due to an obstructed petrol pipe or choked jet.

Engine Knocks

Carburation Failure.

3. Weak mixture, due to incorrect setting or air leaks.

Conditional Failure.

1. Excessive carbon deposit.
2. Insufficient or unsuitable oil.
4. Pre-ignition.

Engine Stops

Carburation Failure.

1. Petrol supply exhausted.
2. Petrol pipe obstructed.
3. Choked jet.
4. Punctured float.
5. Flooded float chamber.
6. Float needle sticking.
14. Air leakage.

Ignition Failure.

16. Broken or dirty plug.
17. Faulty high tension wires.
18. Incorrect ignition timing.
19. Contact breaker arm sticking.
20. Contact breaker points dirty.
21. Contact breaker points maladjusted.
22. Internal shorting due to wet.

Conditional Failure.

7. Poor compression.
11. Gummed piston rings.
12. Sticking valves.
13. Pitted valves.
15. Insufficient oil.

Mechanical Failure.

8. Broken valve.
9. Broken valve spring.
10. Broken or worn piston rings.

In the event of the engine stopping, first of all ascertain whether there is petrol in the tank; if so, check up on the spark at the plug. Next check over the various points in connexion with the carburation system: Petrol pipe obstructed, jet choked, float punctured, float chamber flooded and float needle sticking.

FAULTS AND THEIR DIAGNOSIS

Then test for compression; if poor, the cause will be a broken valve or valve spring, broken piston rings, worn piston rings, gummed piston rings, valve sticking, pitted valve face, air leakage or insufficient oil. If there is no spark at the plug, test for spark at the magneto; this being correct, the cause may be a broken or dirty plug, faulty high tension wire or incorrect magneto timing. If there is no spark at the magneto, this may be due to the contact breaker arm sticking, the points being dirty or maladjusted, or internal shorting due to wet.

INDEX

ADJUSTMENTS, dismantling, etc., 71
—— (mechanical), 90
Amal carburettor, 27
Ammeter, 53
Audible warning of approach, 14
Automatic voltage control, 51, 55

BATTERY, maintenance, 54, 67
Brake adjustment, 85–8

CARBURETTOR controls, 3, 6, 27
Chain adjustment, 81–85
Charging, 55
Clutch, 93, 117
Component parts of the engine, 17
Contact breaker, 58–67
Cycle of four-stroke operations, 24

DECARBONIZING, 113–5
Dismantling rocker box, 109–13
—— —— gear, 105
Driving regulations, 12–16
Dry sump lubrication system, 34
Dynamo, 51
—— brushes, 67

ENGINE lubrication, 34–47
—— troubles, 131
Exhaust valve-lifter, 92

FOUR-stroke engine, 22
Front fork adjustment, 71

GEAR-BOX adjustment, 95
Grinding-in valves, 115

HUB bearings, 75

IGNITION timing, 97

LIGHTING and electrical fittings, 51
Lights, 14

Lubricating bicycle parts, 49
—— dynamo, 68
—— engine, 34
—— gear-box, 46
—— primary chaincase and rear chain, 47

MAGNETO, 18, 58, 67, 69
Mascots, 16

PETROL tap adjustment, 101
Piston removal, 104
Principle of the carburettor, 20

RE-ENAMELLING, 119
Running-in, 9

SIDECAR, alignment, 89
Silencers, 14
Sparking plug, 65, 68
Speed limits, 12
"Speed Twin," dismantling, 110
Spring wheel, 50, 79
Starting-up, 6
Steering, 12, 49, 73
Stopping, 11
Switch positions, 53

TAPPET adjustment, 90, 93
Timing, 97, 99
——, "Magdyno," 98
Traffic regulations, 12
Triumph carburettor, 27
"Twins," 350 c.c., 122
——, —— 500 c.c., 124
Twist-grip, 50, 119
Tyres, 80

VALVE clearances, 90
—— removal, 104, 107, 111, 115

WHEEL bearings, 76–8
Wiring diagrams, 59–62

AUTOBOOKS WORKSHOP MANUALS

ALFA ROMEO GIULIA 1300, 1600, 1750, 2000 1962-1978 WSM
BMW 1600 1966-1973 WSM
BMW 2000 & 2002 1966-1976 WSM
BMW 2500, 2800, 3.0 & 3.3 1968-1977 WSM
BMW 316, 320, 320i 1975-1977 WSM
BMW 518, 520, 520i 1973-1981 WSM
FIAT 1100, 1100D, 1100R & 1200 1957-1969 WSM
FIAT 124 1966-1974 WSM
FIAT 124 SPORT 1966-1975 WSM
FIAT 125 & 125 SPECIAL 1967-1973 WSM
FIAT 126, 126L, 126 DV, 126/650 & 126/650 DV 1972-1982 WSM
FIAT 127 SALOON, SPECIAL & SPORT, 900, 1050 1971-1981 WSM
FIAT 128 1969-1982 WSM
FIAT 1300, 1500 1961-1967 WSM
FIAT 131 MIRAFIORI 1975-1982 WSM
FIAT 132 1972-1982 WSM
FIAT 500 1957-1973 WSM
FIAT 600, 600D & MULTIPLA 1955-1969 WSM
FIAT 850 1964-1972 WSM
JAGUAR E-TYPE 1961-1972 WSM
JAGUAR MK 1, 2 1955-1969 WSM
JAGUAR S TYPE, 420 1963-1968 WSM
JAGUAR XK 120, 140, 150 MK 7, 8, 9 1948-1961 WSM
LAND ROVER 1, 2 1948-1961 WSM
MERCEDES-BENZ 190 1959-1968 WSM
MERCEDES-BENZ 220/8 1968-1972 WSM
MERCEDES-BENZ 220B 1959-1965 WSM
MERCEDES-BENZ 230 1963-1968 WSM
MERCEDES-BENZ 250 1968-1972 WSM
MERCEDES-BENZ 280 1968-1972 WSM
MG MIDGET TA-TF 1936-1955 WSM
MINI 1959-1980 WSM
MORRIS MINOR 1952-1971 WSM
PEUGEOT 404 1960-1975 WSM
PORSCHE 911 1964-1973 WSM
PORSCHE 911 1970-1977 WSM
RENAULT 16 1965-1979 WSM
RENAULT 8, 10, 1100 1962-1971 WSM
ROVER 3500, 3500S 1968-1976 WSM
SUNBEAM RAPIER, ALPINE 1955-1965 WSM
TRIUMPH SPITFIRE, GT6, VITESSE 1962-1968 WSM
TRIUMPH TR2, TR3, TR3A 1952-1962 WSM
TRIUMPH TR4, TR4A 1961-1967 WSM
VOLKSWAGEN BEETLE 1968-1977 WSM

VELOCEPRESS AUTOMOBILE BOOKS & MANUALS

ABARTH BUYERS GUIDE
AUSTIN-HEALEY 6-CYLINDER WSM
AUSTIN-HEALEY SPRITE & MG MIDGET 1958-1971 WSM
BMW 600 LIMOUSINE FACTORY WSM
BMW 600 LIMOUSINE OWNERS HAND BOOK & SERVICE MANUAL
BMW ISETTA FACTORY WSM
BOOK OF THE CARRERA PANAMERICANA - MEXICAN ROAD RACE
COMPLETE CATALOG OF JAPANESE MOTOR VEHICLES
CORVAIR 1960-1969 OWNERS WORKSHOP MANUAL
CORVETTE V8 1955-1962 OWNERS WORKSHOP MANUAL
DIALED IN - THE JAN OPPERMAN STORY
FERRARI 250/GT SERVICE AND MAINTENANCE
FERRARI 308 SERIES BUYER'S AND OWNER'S GUIDE
FERRARI BERLINETTA LUSSO
FERRARI BROCHURES AND SALES LITERATURE 1946-1967
FERRARI BROCHURES AND SALES LITERATURE 1968-1989
FERRARI GUIDE TO PERFORMANCE
FERRARI OPP, MAINTENANCE & SERVICE H/BOOKS 1948-1963
FERRARI OWNER'S HANDBOOK
FERRARI SERIAL NUMBERS PART I - ODD NUMBERS TO 21399
FERRARI SERIAL NUMBERS PART II - EVEN NUMBERS TO 1050
FERRARI SPYDER CALIFORNIA
FERRARI TUNING TIPS & MAINTENANCE TECHNIQUES
HENRY'S FABULOUS MODEL "A" FORD
HOW TO BUILD A FIBERGLASS CAR
HOW TO BUILD A RACING CAR
HOW TO RESTORE THE MODEL 'A' FORD
IF HEMINGWAY HAD WRITTEN A RACING NOVEL
JAGUAR E-TYPE 3.8 & 4.2 WSM
LE MANS 24 (THE BOOK THAT THE FILM WAS BASED ON)
MASERATI BROCHURES AND SALES LITERATURE
MASERATI OWNER'S HANDBOOK
METROPOLITAN FACTORY WSM
MGA & MGB OWNERS HANDBOOK & WSM
OBERT'S FIAT GUIDE
PERFORMANCE TUNING THE SUNBEAM TIGER
PORSCHE 356 1948-1965 WSM
PORSCHE 912 WSM
SOUPING THE VOLKSWAGEN
TRIUMPH TR2, TR3, TR4 1953-1965 WSM
TUNING FOR SPEED (P.E. IRVING)
VEDA ORR'S NEW REVISED HOT ROD PICTORIAL
VOLKSWAGEN TRANSPORTER, TRUCKS, STATION WAGONS WSM
VOLVO 1944-1968 ALL MODELS WSM
WEBER CARBURETORS (EMPHASIS ON ALFA & FIAT)

BROOKLANDS BOOKS & ROAD TEST PORTFOLIOS (RTP)

AC CARS 1904-2009
ALFA ROMEO 1920-1933 ROAD TEST PORTFOLIO
ALFA ROMEO 1934-1940 ROAD TEST PORTFOLIO
BRABHAM RALT HONDA THE RON TAURANAC STORY
BUGATTI TYPE 10 TO TYPE 40 ROAD TEST PORTFOLIO
BUGATTI TYPE 10 TO TYPE 251 ROAD TEST PORTFOLIO
BUGATTI TYPE 41 TO TYPE 55 ROAD TEST PORTFOLIO
BUGATTI TYPE 57 TO TYPE 251 ROAD TEST PORTFOLIO
DELAHAYE ROAD TEST PORTFOLIO
FERRARI ROAD CARS 1946-1956 ROAD TEST PORTFOLIO
FIAT 500 1936-1972 ROAD TEST PORTFOLIO
FIAT DINO ROAD TEST PORTFOLIO
HISPANO SUIZA ROAD TEST PORTFOLIO
HONDA ST1100/ST1300 PAN EUROPEAN 1990-2002 RTP
JAGUAR MK1 & MK2 ROAD TEST PORTFOLIO
LOTUS CORTINA ROAD TEST PORTFOLIO
MV AGUSTA F4 750 & 1000 1997-2007 ROAD TEST PORTFOLIO
TATRA CARS ROAD TEST PORTFOLIO

VELOCEPRESS MOTORCYCLE BOOKS & MANUALS

AJS SINGLES & TWINS 250cc THRU 1000cc 1932-1948 (BOOK OF)
AJS SINGLES 1955-65 350cc & 500cc (BOOK OF)
AJS SINGLES 1945-60 350cc & 500cc MODELS 16 & 18 (BOOK OF)
ARIEL 1939-1960 4 STROKE SINGLES (BOOK OF)
ARIEL LEADER & ARROW 1958-1964 (BOOK OF)
ARIEL MOTORCYCLES 1933-1951 WSM
ARIEL PREWAR MODELS 1932-1939 (BOOK OF)
BMW M/CYCLES R26 R27 (1956-1967) FACTORY WSM
BMW M/CYCLES R50 R50S R60 R69S (1955-1969) FACTORY WSM
BSA BANTAM (BOOK OF)
BSA ALL FOUR-STROKE SINGLES & V-TWINS 1936-1952 (BOOK OF)
BSA OHV & SV SINGLES - 250cc 1954-1970 (BOOK OF)
BSA OHV & SV SINGLES 1945-54 250-600cc (BOOK OF)
BSA OHV SINGLES 350 & 500cc 1955-1967 (BOOK OF)
BSA PRE-WAR MODELS TO 1939 (BOOK OF)
BSA TWINS 1948-1962 (BOOK OF)
BSA TWINS 1962-1969 (SECOND BOOK OF)
CATALOG OF BRITISH MOTORCYCLES (1951 MODELS)
DOUGLAS PRE-WAR ALL MODELS 1929-1939 (BOOK OF)
DOUGLAS POST-WAR ALL MODELS 1948-1957 FACTORY WSM
DUCATI 160cc, 250cc & 350cc OHC MODELS FACTORY WSM
HONDA 50 ALL MODELS UP TO 1970 INC MONKEY & TRAIL (BOOK OF)
HONDA 90 ALL MODELS UP TO 1966 (BOOK OF)
HONDA MOTORCYCLES 125-150 TWINS C/CS/CB/CA WSM
HONDA MOTORCYCLES 250-305 TWINS C/CS/CB WSM
HONDA MOTORCYCLES C100 SUPER CUB WSM
HONDA MOTORCYCLES C110 SPORT CUB 1962-1969 WSM
HONDA TWINS ALL MODELS 125cc THRU 450cc UP TO 1968 (BOOK OF)
INDIAN PONYBIKE, BOY RACER & PAPOOSE ILL PARTS LIST & SALES LIT
J.A.P. ENGINES 1927-1952 & MOTORCYCLES 1934-1952 (BOOK OF)
LAMBRETTA ALL 125 & 150cc MODELS 1947-1957 (BOOK OF)
LAMBRETTA LI & TV MODELS 1957-1970 (SECOND BOOK OF)
MATCHLESS 350 & 500cc SINGLES 1945-1956 (BOOK OF)
MATCHLESS 350 & 500cc SINGLES 1955-1966 (BOOK OF)
NORTON 1932-1947 (BOOK OF)
NORTON 1938-1956 (BOOK OF)
NORTON DOMINATOR TWINS 1955-1965 (BOOK OF)
NORTON MODELS 19, 50 & ES2 1955-1963 (BOOK OF)
NORTON MOTORCYCLES 1957-1970 FACTORY WSM
NORTON PREWAR MODELS 1932-1939 (BOOK OF)
NSU PRIMA ALL MODELS 1956-1964 (BOOK OF)
NSU QUICKLY ALL MODELS 1953-1963 (BOOK OF)
RALEIGH MOPEDS 1960-1969 (BOOK OF)
ROYAL ENFIELD SINGLES & V TWINS 1937-1953 (BOOK OF)
ROYAL ENFIELD SINGLES 1946-1962 (BOOK OF)
ROYAL ENFIELD 736cc INTERCEPTOR FACTORY WSM
ROYAL ENFIELD 250cc & 350cc SINGLES 1958-1966 (SECOND BOOK OF)
SUNBEAM MOTORCYCLES 1928-1939 (BOOK OF)
SUNBEAM S7 & S8 1946-1957 (BOOK OF)
SUZUKI 50cc & 80cc UP TO 1966 (BOOK OF)
SUZUKI T10 1963-1967 FACTORY WSM
SUZUKI T20 & T200 1965-1969 FACTORY WSM
TRIUMPH PRE-WAR MOTORCYCLE 1935-1939 (BOOK OF)
TRIUMPH MOTORCYCLES 1935-1949 (BOOK OF)
TRIUMPH MOTORCYCLES 1937-1951 WSM
TRIUMPH MOTORCYCLES 1945-1955 FACTORY WSM
TRIUMPH TWINS 1945-1958 (BOOK OF)
TRIUMPH TWINS 1956-1969 (BOOK OF)
VELOCETTE ALL SINGLES & TWINS 1925-1970 (BOOK OF)
VESPA 1951-1961 (BOOK OF)
VESPA 125 & 150cc & GS MODELS 1955-1963 (SECOND BOOK OF)
VESPA 90, 125 & 150cc 1963-1972 (THIRD BOOK OF)
VESPA GS & SS 1955-1968 (BOOK OF)
VILLIERS ENGINE (BOOK OF)
VINCENT MOTORCYCLES 1935-1955 WSM

PLEASE VISIT OUR WEBSITE
www.VelocePress.com
FOR A DETAILED DESCRIPTION
OF ANY OF THESE TITLES

www.ingramcontent.com/pod-product-compliance
Lightning Source LLC
Chambersburg PA
CBHW070553170426
43201CB00012B/1821